Embedding Librarianship in Learning Management Systems

Embedding Librarianship in Learning Management Systems

A How-to-Do-It Manual for Librarians

Beth E. Tumbleson and John J. Burke

Chicago 2013

Beth E. Tumbleson is assistant director of the Gardner-Harvey Library, on the Middletown regional campus of Miami University (Ohio). She earned her M.S. in library science from Simmons School of Library Science, M.A. in church history from Trinity Evangelical Divinity School, and B.A. in English and French from Dickinson College. Throughout her career, Beth has worked as an academic, school, and corporate librarian. Beth has co-authored book chapters and journal articles and has co-presented on LMS embedded librarianship at several national conferences including LOEX, ACRL, Off-Campus Library Services, and LITA National Forum as well as at state and regional library conferences and nursing conferences.

John J. Burke is director of the Gardner-Harvey Library on the Middletown regional campus of Miami University (Ohio). He holds an M.S in library science from the University of Tennessee and a B.A. in history from Michigan State University. John's past work experience includes service as both systems/public services librarian and program director for a web-based associate degree in library technology at the University of Cincinnati-Raymond Walters College and also as a reference and electronic resources librarian at Fairmont State College (WV). He has presented on embedded librarianship and a variety of technology topics at ACRL, ALA, the LITA National Forum, LOEX, and various regional and state conferences.

Printed in the United States of America
17 16 15 14 13 5 4 3 2 1

ISBNs: 978-1-55570-862-7 (paper); 978-1-55570-884-9 (PDF); 978-1-55570-885-6 (ePub); 978-1-55570-886-3 (Kindle).

Library of Congress Cataloging-in-Publication Data
Tumbleson, Beth E., 1954–
Embedding librarianship in learning management systems : a how-to-do-it manual for librarians / Beth E. Tumbleson and John J. Burke.
pages cm
Includes bibliographical references and index.
ISBN 978-1-55570-862-7 (alk. paper)
1. Academic libraries—Relations with faculty and curriculum. 2. Academic librarians—Professional relationships. 3. Information literacy—Study and teaching (Higher) 4. Libraries and colleges—United States—Case studies. I. Burke, John (John J.) II. Title.
Z675.U5T86 2013
025.5′677—dc23 2013005369

This paper meets the requirements of ANSI/NISO Z39.48–1992 (Permanence of Paper).

This work is dedicated with love to my husband Gary, children Jeffrey and Janelle, and parents Philip and Virginia Dennett, who are lifelong learners and supporters of libraries.

—Beth E. Tumbleson

I would like to thank my wife Lynne and children Madeline, Anna, Philip, and Andrew, my parents, and my in-laws.

—John J. Burke

Contents

Preface

Welcome to *Embedding Librarianship in Learning Management Systems: A How-to-Do-It Manual.* This work is all about collaborating with faculty and engaging with students at the point where they begin their research: in their learning management system (LMS) classroom. This book begins a conversation between the authors and the reader in which the LMS embedded librarian experience and best practices will be shared. In return, the authors hope that you will gain knowledge, skills, and insights and will develop or further refine your own embedded program. The authors look forward to hearing your stories of battle for information literacy in the LMS and about your ultimate success. Whether you are already working with classes in your LMS or considering how to begin a pilot, this manual offers guidance and encouragement to academic librarians. You will find questions to ask, examples to explore, tools to use, and best practices to implement in these pages.

The book is based on the authors' first-hand implementation of LMS embedded librarian services on their campus and undergirded by the professional literature where librarians publish their findings and experiences. Through the process of investigating embedded librarianship, conducting a pilot, and expanding the program, the authors connected with colleagues across the continent who were pioneering in tough terrain and with innovators who were experimenting with emerging technologies and new techniques. The authors are convinced that LMS embedded librarianship is becoming the primary and most productive method for connecting with college and university students, who are increasingly mobile and concerned with course materials and requirements delivered in the LMS. The book includes our rationale for this approach and much practical guidance to get your embedded librarian service up and running smoothly.

The human factor is the heart of LMS embedded librarianship, although embedded librarians are often swept up in technology issues. The "new" creates great excitement in the minds of many. Commercial vendors introduce emerging technologies, which are then promoted in trade journals, and later analyzed by information and technology professionals at conferences and online. Various angles of the hardware, software, and the market are discussed. Learning management systems are no different. As they are developed, new tools and improved features are made available to enhance teaching and learning. Unfortunately, end users engaged in interacting with one another can be overlooked by developers and marketing magnets.

This focus on the human factor, of supporting the teaching, learning, and research mission on a campus, is the librarian's forte. For decades, public service librarians have staffed service desks to assist users with their questions related to finding answers and building their knowledge base. Reference librarians engage the individual, listen, discover what is wanted, and seek to point the stakeholder in profitable directions. Instruction librarians, in contrast, step into the classroom and attempt to lead a group of students in new ways of searching for wanted information. Sometimes that instruction librarian even designs curriculum and teaches his own credit course to guide information seekers in the ways of finding, evaluating, and using information published in various formats. Librarians also work in systems, emerging technologies, and digital initiatives in order to provide the infrastructure or improve access to collections and services for end users through the library website, discovery layers, etc. Although these arenas seemingly differ, librarians work as one when they consider foremost the human dimension, the real needs of students, staff, and faculty on campus. This is a librarian's training and mindset: People matter most.

This, then, is the impetus of undertaking LMS embedded librarianship. Academic librarians who are familiar with their library collections, trained in conducting academic research and its tools, and are comfortable interacting with novice and experienced scholars are ideally suited to share expertise in the single online arena where instructor, students, and librarian may meet to foster intellectual inquiry and empower others in information-seeking. Members of today's campus community may bypass the physical library as they rush from classroom to laboratory to cafeteria. Still, there are research intensive periods when undergraduates and graduate students alike are very much in need of an approachable guide who is able and willing to recommend research strategies, library services, and potential resources at the institution and through interlibrary loan or the state's library consortia.

The LMS makes this meeting easier, more personal, and highly probable since this is the designated space for academic interchange. Working as an LMS embedded librarian is both a proactive approach to library instruction using available technologies and enabling a 24/7 presence. It literally provides access to library collections and services day and night and around the world. Yes, it is a new approach to an old mission: offering information expertise and assistance in research upon request. It is a service valued by those who spend time online and are actively teaching and learning there. It seems obvious that librarians must collaborate with faculty to gain entrance to this LMS world of intellectual engagement. Librarians' understanding of the ways knowledge is produced, organized, stored, and distributed enlightens and empowers lifelong learners. Once end users understand that interacting with library professionals can be useful, and that librarians are willing to impart practical skills in a world of complex information, students welcome librarians. Soon, they become trusted partners in learning, and then they are invited inside previously closed doors. They are asked to contribute ideas and redesign research assignments to strengthen information literacy. At least, this has been the authors' experience. It is our sincere hope it will become yours as well.

Embedding Librarianship in Learning Management Systems: A How-to-Do-It Manual contains 9 chapters:

- Chapter 1, "An Introduction to Embedded Librarianship," offers a definition of embedded librarianship and draws on the professional literature to compare various methods of information literacy instruction with embedded librarianship and to show the need for this approach.
- Chapter 2, "The Embedded Librarian and the LMS," provides an overview of the LMS and identifies the tools available to the embedded librarian.
- Chapter 3, "Creating a Pilot Program," details a step-by-step approach to creating a pilot LMS embedded librarian program on your campus.

- Chapter 4, "Marketing LMS Embedded Librarianship," covers the process of promoting embedded librarian services to gain new faculty collaborators and to encourage student buy-in and usage.
- Chapter 5, "Building the Embedded Librarian Presence: Instructional Content and Instructional Design," creates a model for approaching the research needs of a given course or assignment and identifying the proper content to include, with special guidance on creating custom materials.
- Chapter 6, "Online, Face-to-Face, and Hybrid Courses," compares the different types of classes that can benefit from an embedded librarian's contributions and provides tips for interacting with students in each setting.
- Chapter 7, "Assessing the Impact of Embedded Librarians," identifies methods for measuring the effectiveness of the embedded librarian service and the information literacy skills of participating students.
- Chapter 8, "Extending Your Reach While Coping with Workload Issues," calls on librarians to pause and assess their library programs and priorities, noting the impact on day-to-day workflow, before increasing their investment in embedded librarianship.
- Chapter 9, "Future Developments in Embedded Librarianship," recommends methods for librarians to stay informed of best practices in LMS embedded librarianship while remaining current on changes in higher education and technology that make an even stronger argument for adopting embedded work.

Finally, an appendix that presents results from the LMS Embedded Librarian Survey, a comprehensive bibliography of both cited and recommended sources for more information, and a helpful index to topics discussed throughout the book are included.

Join the growing community of LMS embedded librarians and contribute to the expanding experience and body of knowledge on the embedded librarians in the LMS discussion list that can be subscribed to at http://listserv.muohio.edu/archives/emlibs.html. Please direct any questions or comments to the authors at EmbeddedLibrarianship@gmail.com.

Acknowledgments

We would both like to express appreciation to the library staff at the Gardner-Harvey Library, who enable us to innovate and work productively. We are grateful to colleagues throughout the profession who are leading the way in LMS embedded librarianship and have shared their expertise and experiences with generosity. We celebrate the Miami University faculty, who have collaborated with us by allowing us to embed in their LMS courses and to interact with their students to strengthen information literacy. Special thanks are due to Rob Schorman for supporting our professional development, Janet Hurn for providing leadership in e-learning on campus, Ellenmarie Wahlrab for coordinating the Center for Teaching and Learning, and Carolyn Mason for giving free reign in her nursing LMS courses to the extent of redesigning assignments and presenting at nursing conferences. We are privileged to engage Miami University students in the LMS, in the classroom, and at the library InfoDesk as they pursue scholarly research and move forward with their academic and professional goals. Based on these rewarding relationships, it was possible to write this book and share the learning and teaching vision with readers. Finally, we thank Neal-Schuman Publishers, who encouraged us in the project and especially our editors, Sandy Wood and Patrick Hogan, for their patience and attention to a myriad of details which resulted in a finer publication. Above all, we return thanks to God who bestows blessings daily: life, community, and work which we share herein. Shalom.

An Introduction to LMS Embedded Librarianship

IN THIS CHAPTER:

LMS Embedded Librarianship

The term "embedded" has been applied to journalists who accompany troops into battle. These embedded outsiders gain a firsthand look at experiences that might otherwise only be visible to or communicated by participants. Applying this metaphor to the academic realm, students and faculty are the firsthand participants in courses, completing and assigning work, interacting about course content and requirements, and experiencing the highs and lows of the learning process. When librarians are consulted by students with research assignment questions or asked by a faculty member to provide a library instruction session for a course, they are brought inside the veil for a time. They see the course in part, but not in whole. The librarians' participation is mediated by others who have seen the assignment or course topics in the context of a larger study. By being embedded, librarians might gain a clearer, more accurate view.

Embeddedness involves more than just gaining perspective. It also allows the outsider to become part of the group through shared learning experiences and goals. The embedded librarian develops a sense of partnership, participation, and community with students and faculty, who recognize the value of librarians and librarianship. In this way, each group develops greater trust and respect for the other. No longer does the library remain a faceless support entity at the periphery of teacher and student interactions; now an available librarian can be relied on for research assistance. While she may be neither fish nor fowl, neither student nor instructor, the embedded librarian becomes an active participant in the course.

History

Before we begin exploring embedded librarianship in the learning management system (LMS) in earnest, it is helpful to understand the origins and larger context of embedded librarianship. The concept of embedded librarianship includes other types of collaboration between librarians and information-seekers. It is difficult to trace the precise origins of the term, but Shumaker and Tyler provide an excellent overview of its development and uses in their 2007 study. They cite articles by Davenport and Prusak (1993) and Bauwens (1993) that encouraged special librarians to get out of the library and into close contact with those who needed their services. These suggestions on becoming involved more directly in the work of researchers were joined to an even earlier movement in medical librarianship, pioneered by Gertrude Lamb in the early 1970s, which placed clinical librarians on medical teams to supply information to physicians as they made rounds (Lipscomb 2000).

The first use of the phrase "embedded librarian" in print was by Barbara Dewey (2004), who outlined various ways that academic librarians can strategically collaborate on campus. Embedded librarianship in this larger sense takes many forms in an academic setting. There are ways to be embedded physically among the students and faculty one serves, such as the placement of a librarian in a discipline-related classroom or laboratory building or near faculty offices. Historically, there have been branch libraries on college and university campuses that represent this sort of embedding, although they generally include a dedicated physical space and a print material collection (Drewes and Hoffman 2010). A librarian can also embed in the workflow or task process of campus groups by serving as a member of a scientific research group, a team of educators and technologists bringing digital resources into existence, or a faculty learning community. On the instructional side, librarians have participated in regular class meetings for courses (both in person and via Twitter). Dewey also points to librarians participating in campus governance and in campus fundraising efforts (2004), in both cases to connect librarians and libraries to broader campus efforts. Kesselman and Watstein (2010) add the involvement of libraries in scholarly communication activities, creating metadata and creating digital spaces for scholarship.

Components

Embedded librarianship in the LMS is all about being as close as possible to where students are receiving their assignments and gaining instruction and advice from faculty members. Rather than the geographical closeness implied by the embedded methods listed above, this mode recognizes the centrality of the LMS for coursework delivery and class interaction on many campuses. Another metaphor for embedded librarians that fits their online presence is the concept of embedding a video so that it plays right on a web page (rather than linking out to another page or site on which to view it) or embedding a widget on a web page to allow a patron to search a database or instant message (IM) the library (Drewes and Hoffman 2010). Embedding a librarian in the LMS gives the librarian full (or nearly full) access to course materials and course tools. This provides the information a librarian needs to understand course research needs and deadlines and also the means to share information resources and information literacy guidance with students.

The first publication chronicling the appearance of a librarian embedded in an LMS dates from 2001 (Dorner 2001). The initial Blackboard posting of information literacy tutorials for nursing students has inspired a variety of approaches for reaching out to students and recommending resources (see Cox 2002, for another early approach to embedding in the LMS). The embedded model in the LMS today allows for the use of a broad palette of LMS tools and library service offerings. Many detailed descriptions of individual libraries' embedded programs exist in the literature, and several of them will appear throughout the remaining chapters of the book.

The growth of diverse methods in embedded librarianship has been a highly adaptive process. Librarians have joined faculty members in adopting new features and capabilities that are added within the LMS and also strategically lobbying for their creation. Another key approach for librarians has been to follow the paths trod by the participants in each course: the tools they use are the tools the embedded librarian also chooses. There are often chances to guide students and faculty to adapt their thinking as well by introducing a new tool or use of the LMS.

A Survey of LMS Embedded Librarians

To give you an overview of some common aspects and activities, the authors conducted a survey of embedded librarians in September 2011 by posting a link to the survey on several library discussion groups (see sidebar for a list of the groups, and see the appendix for a lengthier summary of the survey results). The survey included the question, "What does embedded librarianship include at your institution?" Below is a list of the responses ranked by their frequency of use among the 280 survey respondents (showing the number of respondents who chose that response and their percentage of total respondents; respondents were encouraged to mark all applicable responses).

- Encouragement to contact the embedded librarian for further reference assistance (203)—76 percent
- Links to library databases and other information resources within the course (202)—76 percent
- Individual librarian assigned to one or more participating courses (195)—73 percent
- Library tab or link to the library website in the LMS for all courses (193)—72 percent
- Tutorials, either embedded or linked, in the course (184)—69 percent
- Information on research concepts (i.e., scholarly vs. popular periodicals, plagiarism, citing sources) (177)—66 percent
- Suggested research strategies for course assignments (168)—63 percent
- Instant messaging or chat widgets in the course (69)—26 percent
- Interactive sessions with classes using web conferencing software (Adobe Connect, Elluminate, Wimba, WebEx, etc.) (57)—21 percent
- Synchronous chats with groups of students (37)—14 percent

These results reveal that among the group surveyed most already have a tab or link in their LMS that leads students to the library website. Those practicing embedded librarianship in the LMS tend toward assigning an individual librarian to each course. That librarian is responsible for offering reference assistance and contact information, providing links to additional resources related to the course, and including access to tutorials, coverage of information literacy concepts, and course-related search strategies. All of these findings correspond well to the image of embedded librarianship presented in the literature and the type of program that this book will prepare you to build at your institution. Of course, there are many unique combinations of services that a given library could employ, so there should be no fear of falling into lockstep with the majority view or unimaginatively "keeping up with the Joneses."

A total of 201 respondents (72 percent) currently have librarians embedded in LMS courses, while 23 (8 percent) have had librarians embedded in the past. The remaining 20 percent were interested in starting such a service. Of the embedded programs, 48 percent had begun from one to four years ago, with 15 percent just having begun in the last 12 months and 18 percent existing for more than four years. Positive comments from the respondents' institutions included these two: "They like that the information is in their courses and they don't have to go looking for it," and "Students appreciate having direct access to the librarian who taught their session and is familiar with their assignment/prof requirements."

Further responses from the survey offer a sense of the scope of embedded librarianship. Of the respondents surveyed, 55 percent are located at universities offering graduate degrees and 23 percent are from community colleges, with the remaining 22 percent coming from a mix of four-year colleges and universities, university regional campuses, and for-profit institutions. While respondents were overwhelmingly from institutions in the United States, responses came from librarians in Abu Dhabi, Australia, Canada, England, India, Italy, Jamaica, Malaysia, Mexico, New Zealand, Scotland, and Spain. More data from the survey will be shared in the succeeding chapters (and in summary form in the appendix), but it is clear that embedded librarianship is growing, has elements that appeal to its desired audience, and is a worldwide phenomenon.

Library Discussion Groups Where the Survey Was Posted

- academic_division@sla.lyris.net (Special Libraries Association Academic Division)
- alao@lists.uakron.edu (Academic Library Association of Ohio)
- cjc-1@ala.org (ACRL Community and Junior Colleges Section)
- COLLIB-L@ala.org (ACRL College Libraries Section)
- ili-1@ala.org (ACRL Information Literacy Section)
- infolit@ala.org (American Library Association (ALA) Information Literacy Discussion List)
- LIS-INFOLITERACY@JISCMAIL.AC.UK (Chartered Institute of Library and Information Professionals (CILIP) Information Literacy Group)
- lita-1@ala.org (Library Information Technology Association)
- OCLSCONF@ls2.cmich.edu (Past and present attendees of the Distance Library Services Conference)
- OFFCAMP@listserv.utk.edu (Association of College and Research Libraries (ACRL) Distance Library Services Section)
- ohiolink@lists.ohiolink.edu (OhioLINK Consortium)
- univers@infoserv.inist.fr (International Federation of Library Associations and Institutions (IFLA) Academic and Research Libraries Section)

LMS Embedded Librarianship Is the Solution

> [I]f we are to remain responsive to our users' diverse information, reference, and research needs, we envision a future in which embedded librarians—and embedded librarianship—are

> the norm rather than at the forefront. (Kesselman and Watstein 2009, 395–396).

Embedded librarianship occurs in the online space familiar to students who log in daily for coursework. LMS embedded librarianship is distinguished from other modes of instruction in that it delivers relevant library resources and services needed by students grappling with course-specific research assignments in the campus LMS. When embedded librarians provide ready access to scholarly electronic collections, research databases, and Web 2.0 tools and tutorials, the research experience becomes less frustrating and more focused for students. Undergraduates associate this familiar online environment with the academic world. They may conveniently login 24/7. Getting started becomes easier for those uncertain how and where to begin research and feeling overwhelmed by so much digital information. By collaborating with faculty, embedded librarians are able to convert traditional methods of instruction to the LMS and maximize delivering research instruction to students as needed.

Maximizes Instructional Efforts

Traditional information literacy instruction has incorporated such methods as the reference desk, research consultations, one-shot instruction sessions, credit courses, and the library website. Through these time-tested, instructional outlets, users who reached out to librarians received research assistance. In contrast, LMS embedded librarianship uses a more proactive and long-term approach to transform the standard fare of instruction.

Reference Services

Reference librarians have traditionally been stationed at public service desks to await patrons who approach with questions. Users are comfortable asking directional questions concerning the photocopier location, library hours, or where a title can be found in the stacks, but are often reluctant to pose in-depth research questions. According to the ERIAL (Ethnographic Research in Illinois Academic Libraries) Project, a two-year, five-campus study, students first seek research help from their professors or peers. After all, the instructor is the subject expert who designed the assignment and will grade it. Students do not typically seek out librarians as research consultants, even when virtual reference services are offered. "Although the majority of IWU

[Illinois Wesleyan University] students struggled with finding the correct database to use, their search terms, locating a known item, and /or technical problems, not one student sought the assistance of a librarian during an observed search" (Asher and Duke 2012b, 83). Librarians speculate as to why reference desk usage has fallen off so drastically.

> Many of the articles discussed the possible influences on the decline of reference desk statistics. Major trends in the suggestions are the users' assumed familiarity with Internet searching and the growth of distance education courses, allowing students to use their local libraries rather than the library of the school offering the course or degree. The reticence of users to admit that they need help may also contribute to the decline, especially as many users feel that web-based products should be as easy to use as their favorite search engine and become easily frustrated when this is not true. (Thomsett-Scott and Reese 2006, 151)

Problem-solving library administrators are reassessing the staffing of these service points to maximize the impact of professional librarians. Some library directors have attempted to address this decline and librarian-student disconnect by having reference librarians circulate through the library building with portable iPads or by providing incoming undergraduates with a "personal librarian," as they do at Drexel University, where each librarian is assigned 100 students to guide (Oder and Blumenstein 2010). Given current budget cuts and reduced traffic at the reference desk, some are deciding to staff reference with student assistants and/or library support staff, combine public service desks, or even close the reference desk.

A more productive approach to providing information literacy instruction is to proactively show up as embedded librarians in the online learning space faculty and students already frequent. LMS embedded librarianship addresses these troubling issues through partnership with the professor. Once the embedded librarian is endorsed as a valued information expert by the instructor, she becomes an approachable member of the course from the students' perspective. Next, the librarian becomes informed about assignment details and recommends research strategies and sources to students in their LMS course. Reference assistance is actively delivered online and within the course, where students prefer to conduct research. Once aware of a research obstacle encountered by one student, the embedded librarian can then use the LMS e-mail tool to notify the entire class with timely search solutions by offering links to named electronic resources. Helping a whole class search effectively can be as easy as assisting one student. As trust develops between students and the embedded librarian, they are more likely to seek out that librarian's help at the reference desk. Often this research relationship continues from semester to semester.

Research Consultations

Research consultations between a student and librarian provide the necessary individualized assistance some students seek. They are ideal for students working on capstone projects and theses, but are also valuable for first year or non-traditional students. Unfortunately, those who stand to benefit do not always request a librarian's assistance. Faculty report that students are shocked to discover a librarian will meet with them (Armstrong 2012, 45). Some students are unaware that librarians are trained information specialists: "Our participant students did not always think of librarians as individuals with research expertise" (Miller and Murillo 2012, 55).

LMS embedded librarianship enables librarians to introduce themselves to students within the LMS course framework and market their research services. The librarian may easily arrange a consultation with students who e-mail, IM, text, call, or drop-in. Sometimes, instructors will require research consultations with the embedded librarian or offer extra credit to motivate students to work with the collaborating librarian. A professor's encouragement makes a world of difference to students and the embedded librarian.

One-Shot Library Instruction Sessions

Some faculty request one-shot information literacy sessions, either because they respect librarians' search experience and bibliographic knowledge, or because the institution requires the incorporation of information literacy into the curriculum. These sessions usually are limited in time from 50 to 75 minutes. Students who participate in these sessions, however, may hesitate to raise issues connected with their topics, due to limited time or to preserve their image before peers. Timing the session can be an issue. If it is offered too early in the term, elements are forgotten by students, or if it is offered too close to the assignment deadline, other students may have already completed the research assignment.

LMS embedded librarianship extends the benefits of one-shots. Often, instructors collaborating with an embedded librarian request a one-shot class so students have the opportunity to practice search techniques with a librarian physically present. This may also happen virtually in online courses, using synchronous software for group instruction. Thus, a crossover between virtual and face-to-face is not uncommon in embedded librarianship.

Follow-up instruction may also ensue. The librarian may post or send students additional tools or strategies at appropriate intervals prior to due dates. Having taught students face-to-face in a computer lab, embedded librarians are aware of the usual pitfalls students encounter narrowing a topic, searching, or citing sources. Anticipating these difficulties, they embed appropriate content. Students may solicit help privately through the LMS e-mail or chat tools, or publicly by posting to a course discussion board or forum. Students may eventually come to rely on librarians as part of their research process. According to the ERIAL Project, some faculty would welcome this integrated library content: "Teaching faculty often expressed a willingness to integrate instructional content into their courses to reinforce the outcomes of a library instruction session" (Armstrong 2012, 40). In this way, more extensive information literacy instruction can be provided.

> An ongoing presence by a librarian offers a clear advantage over the typical one-time visits by librarians that are common in face-to-face courses. In the online setting with an embedded librarian students receive support when they need it. They ask questions and receive information when it's relevant to what they are doing in the course. They are also more likely to seek help when the librarian is integrated into the course, Klinger says. ("Team Teaching" 2008, 6)

Information Literacy Credit Courses

When a librarian offers a for-credit course in information literacy, whether as a general introduction or as a discipline-specific research methods course, she is able to set the learning outcomes and curriculum rather than accommodating a professor's objectives. A for-credit course allows sufficient time to cover a wide array of finding tools, explore a variety of electronic resources, apply search strategies, and synthesize concepts in scholarly communication.

As the librarian lectures, leads discussions, and oversees in-class practicums and student presentations, she sets the pace and establishes relationships with students. Credit-bearing information literacy courses may also be offered entirely online, using modules where students cover concepts and complete exercises. Unfortunately, only a limited number of students may enroll in each section of an elective course. Those sections are also limited in reach by the number of librarians available to teach each term. There may be uneven coverage of research methods courses among the various academic disciplines. Required introductory courses may also lack contextual ties to any discipline.

LMS embedded librarianship addresses these shortcomings by providing relevant research strategies and resources students will need to complete the specific course assignments, whatever the course level, format, or subject. If the embedded librarian has taken the time to develop a full credit course curriculum, he may reformat that content in a just-in-time approach for the LMS courses in which he is embedded. Indeed, the most significant modules or tutorials can readily be copied, embedded, or linked in any number of LMS courses by the embedded librarian so that students learn how to conduct academic research. This extends the embedded librarian's reach of introducing students to the necessary research strategies and accessing the most relevant library collections.

Library Website

The clear strength of the library website is its accessibility. The online catalog, research databases, interactive research guides or LibGuides, digital tutorials, and Web 2.0 tools can be readily linked and made available 24/7. Unfortunately, few searchers begin here. According to Steven J. Bell, the library website is no longer considered by faculty and students as the gateway to the electronic riches necessary for scholarly research.

> Put simply, the library portal as we know it today is unsustainable. It, along with a host of other indicators such as declines in reference questions and shifts from print to e-resources, signals that for academic libraries a 'let's just keep doing business as usual' mentality is a sure path to obsolescence. (Bell 2009)

According to an OCLC survey, "84 percent of the total respondents begin their search for information using a search engine; no respondents begin at the library Web site" (OCLC 2010). Regrettably, the website layout may also confuse students: "In comparison with the ease of the Google user experience, the various and fragmented catalogs, databases, and interfaces contained on a typical academic library's website are extremely complex" (Asher and Duke 2012b, 72).

Even when students navigate the library website, they may overlook potentially helpful screencasts buried on an unnoticed page. Novice researchers do not imagine subject guides are available and located on the library homepage. Students scanning an alphabetical list of databases, moreover, may not recognize which ones among the many are best suited to their research topics. Although scholarly content is organized and accessed at the library website, students do not necessarily reap the benefits of the academic library collection, which comprises a considerable percentage of its budget.

LMS embedded librarians streamline the plethora of proprietary databases and finding tools by placing them within students' LMS courses or next to the research assignment itself. In this way, scholarly resources, subject guides, and learning objects on the library website pages become visible to students getting started and are used more readily. Nor do students have to choose from among databases and learning objects, since the embedded librarian posts and links the most applicable ones, saving student's research time for other tasks.

Resolves Dilemmas Documented in the Library Literature

> Many—not all—educators are failing to teach students how to navigate a vast wilderness of information—to discern what they can trust, edit out what is unnecessary, redundant or unreliable, and focus on what they really need. (Head and Eisenberg 2011)

The library literature illuminates the new paradigm and underscores the timely solution that embedded librarianship represents. In 2008, lead investigators Alison J. Head and Michael B. Eisenberg began conducting the University of Washington national research study called Project Information Literacy (PIL). This involved surveying and interviewing "more than 10,000 U.S. students at 31 colleges and universities, including undergraduates enrolled at UW, Harvard, Ohio State University, University of Michigan and community colleges, such as Shoreline Community College" (Head and Eisenberg 2011). In 2010, Head and Eisenberg released two progress reports; one focused on faculty: *Assigning Inquiry: How Handouts for Research Assignments Guide Today's College Students,* and the other on undergraduates: *Truth Be Told: How College Students Evaluate and Use Information in the Digital Age.*

What becomes disturbingly clear is that faculty focus on the mechanics of the research paper over the research process. "Six in 10 handouts recommended students consult the library shelves—a placed-based source—more than scholarly research databases, the library catalog, the Web, or for that matter, any other resources. Only 13 percent of the handouts suggested consulting a librarian for assistance with research" (Head and Eisenberg 2010a, 3). Undergraduates seek guidance primarily from their professors when conducting research for course assignments. Although students are using libraries, 70 percent avoid librarians. Head and Eisenberg observe, "Librarians were tremendously underutilized by students. Eight out of 10 of the respondents reported rarely, if ever, turning to librarians for help with course-related research assignments" (Head and Eisenberg 2009, 3). Sadly, librarians were listed near the bottom of most PIL survey charts tabulating whom students consult in research. Head and Eisenberg conclude by urging academic librarians to "take an active role and initiate the dialogue with faculty to close a divide that may be growing between them and faculty and between them and students" and caution that experiences will differ among campuses (Head and Eisenberg 2009, 34–35).

Students today are not slackers "tethered to Facebook and their smartphones on their way to another party" (Head and Eisenberg 2011). In *Truth Be Told,* Head and Eisenberg confirm undergraduates are motivated to pass the course, complete assignments, and get good grades (Head and Eisenberg 2010b, 4). At the same time, they acknowledge students are facing an unfamiliar information terrain, information overload, or "the sense of being inundated by all the resources at their disposal" (Head and Eisenberg 2009, 9). PIL findings document that undergraduates are confused, frustrated, and likely to procrastinate. Head and Eisenberg identify four research contexts with which undergraduates struggle: big picture, language, situational context, and information gathering (Head and Eisenberg 2009, 4). They observe that "eight in 10 of our 8,353 respondents reported having overwhelming difficulty even starting research assignments and determining the nature and scope of what was expected of them. Nearly half of the students in our survey sample experienced nagging uncertainty about how to conclude and assess the quality of their research efforts" (Head and Eisenberg 2011). In order to cope, students draw upon "a small set of familiar, tried-and-true resources, which infrequently includes librarians, for completing one assignment to the next" (Head and Eisenberg 2010b, 35). Additionally, "[a]lmost all respondents used a Google search, at some point, during their research process—but not always first or to the exclusion of using other sources (for example, course readings, scholarly research databases, or Wikipedia)" (Head and Eisenberg 2009, 15).

The ERIAL Project corroborates PIL findings in its publication *Libraries and Student Culture: What We Now Know.* To summarize, librarians are underutilized by students, who "do not necessarily ask librarians for help. Library literature suggests that students have a limited understanding of what librarians can do for them" (Miller and Murillo 2012, 50); they "rarely ask librarians for help, even when they need it. The idea of a librarian as an academic expert who is available to talk about assignments and hold their hands through the research process in, in fact, foreign to most students" (Kolowich 2011). Neither were ERIAL researchers impressed by students' information literacy abilities: "Almost without exception, Illinois Wesleyan University (IWU) students exhibited a lack of understanding of search logic, how to build a search to narrow or expand results, how to use subject headings, and how various search engines (including Google) organize and display results" (Asher and Duke, 2012b: 76). The Illinois researchers also found librarians and faculty contribute to the problem by overestimating students' research skills, which intimidates students. By embedding in the LMS, a librarian anticipates students' research questions and provides instruction that will be needed. Proactive LMS embedded librarianship is the solution to the problems identified in these studies.

> If librarians wish to remain relevant in today's world, the profession must continue to actively seek ways to engage more deeply in the academic community. Sitting passively at the reference desk, waiting for students and faculty to find us, is no longer a sustainable model. (Asher and Duke 2012a, 167)

Faculty Research Behavior, PIL Findings

- Emphasize research paper mechanics: format, length, style
- Don't explain research process or its rationale
- Refer students to library shelves
- Only 13 percent of handouts suggest students consult a librarian
- Instructors with 5 or fewer years of teaching experience include fewest references to information sources from library

(Head and Eisenberg 2010a)

Undergraduate Research Behavior, PIL Findings

- Like easy, predictable research
- Prefer anything online
- Use a few, familiar resources
- Rely on high school habits
- 84 percent have a hard time starting
- 83 percent use course readings, Google, research databases, faculty
- Want detailed guidance from faculty
- Want the professor to assign narrowed topic
- Don't realize intellectual inquiry takes time and thought nor appreciate its value

(Head and Eisenberg 2010b)

LMS Embedded Librarianship Makes Information Literacy Accessible

> Locating and evaluating information is an essential skill for academic success. Moreover, the ability to conduct a successful and efficient search for high-quality information is a critical thinking skill that is central to live in contemporary information and knowledge-driven environments. (Asher and Duke 2012b, 71)

Today's academic libraries remain open 24/7 virtually. Twenty-first century librarians engage in scholarly research, collection development, teaching, instructional design, and information technology. These skills and experience transfer well to the LMS environment where users opt to start research. Student-centered librarians who desire to interact with them need to be in the LMS, too. Embedded librarianship embraces these new opportunities to disseminate knowledge electronically, globally, and immediately in the age-old quest to promote teaching and learning. Learners today are no longer bound by the prior limits of physical space, time, and access. Their information landscape has become simultaneously larger and more complex as publishing paradigms shift from print to electronic and from proprietary to open access, and content is no longer place-bound but accessible on mobile devices. Many users need an information specialist who will provide instruction in information literacy so they may pursue their academic and professional goals. At the same time, LMS embedded librarianship takes advantage of a user's preference to work electronically and independently.

The plethora of information sources available online and their relative ease of access give students a sense of autonomy and self-control that feels liberating and empowering. Librarians can work with this sense of self-efficacy by weaving our presence into their online world via chat reference, online guides and tutorials, and other tools that will connect them to the library from where they are already connected (Miller and Murillo 2012, 68–69).

When embedded librarians arrive in the LMS and offer research solutions to students in need, the work of embedded librarianship is appreciated and seen as value-added.

A 21st Century Skill

> Information literacy is the essential skill set that cuts across all disciplines and professions. (Head and Eisenberg 2011)

More than 90 organizations recognize the significance of information literacy (http://infolit.org/supporters) and have written it into their mission statements. In 1989, the American Library Association established the National Forum on Information Literacy (NFIL) to advocate for information literacy. It celebrated its twentieth anniversary on October 15, 2011. Within academic librarianship, the Association of College and Research Libraries (ACRL) of the American Library Association is the body that governs information literacy standards. In 2000, these standards were approved by the ACRL Board of Directors to guide academic librarians instructing their campus in information literacy. They were also approved in 1999 by the American Association for Higher Education and in 2004 by the Council for Independent Colleges. The standards may be used in various instructional venues by academic librarians.

Applying LMS Embedded Librarianship to the ACRL Standards

> LMS embedded librarianship is an effective means to sensitize students to information literacy standards. ERIAL findings reveal students struggle with the nature and evaluation of information and that they "also exhibited a lack of understanding of where the border is located between library resources and Internet resources." (Asher and Duke 2012b, 82)

In accordance with ACRL Standards One and Three, librarians might engage students who rely on their smartphones, while keeping in mind that "[s]tudents who retrieve information on their smartphones may also have trouble understanding or evaluating how the information on their phone is 'produced, organized, and disseminated' (Standard One)" (Yarmey-Tylutki 2010, 14). As for Standard Two, which deals with effective search strategies, the LMS embedded librarian must go beyond Boolean operators and controlled vocabulary, since emerging technologies incorporate new means of searching.

Information Literacy Organizations

- American Association of School Librarians. Standards and Guidelines—www.ala.org/aasl/guidelinesandstandards/guidelinesandstandards
- American Association of School Librarians. AASL Standards for the 21st-Century Learner—www.ala.org/aasl/guidelinesandstandards/learningstandards/standards
- Association of College and Research Libraries. American Library Association. Information Literacy Competency Standards for Higher Education—www.ala.org/ala/mgrps/divs/acrl/standards/informationliteracycompetency.cfm
- Association of American Colleges and Universities. Information Literacy VALUE Rubric—www.aacu.org/value/rubrics/pdf/InformationLiteracy.pdf
- National Forum on Information Literacy—www.infolit.org
- Partnership for 21st Century Skills—www.p21.org
- Project Information Literacy—http://projectinfolit.org
- Society of College, National and University Libraries. The Seven Pillars of Information Literacy—www.sconul.ac.uk/groups/information_literacy/seven_pillars.html
- UNESCO. Towards Media and Information Literacy Indicators—www.unesco.org/new/fileadmin/MULTIMEDIA/HQ/CI/CI/pdf/unesco_mil_indicators_background_document_2011_final_en.pdf

> However, smartphones defy this focus on word-based searching and instead offer several novel methods of search. Smartphone-owning students can use a variety of input types—photographs, QR codes, barcodes, sounds, spoken words, and even their geographical location—to retrieve customized information relevant to their current situation. This developing world of mobile search places an onus on librarians to understand emerging search strategies and incorporate them into our information literacy instruction where needed. (Yarmey-Tylutki 2010, 14)

Instructors often request librarians to address Standard Five, the ethical and legal use of information. LMS embedded librarians may link to citation generators and LibGuides on citing sources according to the American Psychological Association or the Modern Language Association citation styles, or provide tutorials on preventing plagiarism.

ACRL Standards

1. The information literate student determines the nature and extent of the information needed.
2. The information literate student accesses needed information effectively and efficiently.
3. The information literate student evaluates information and its sources critically and incorporates selected information into his or her knowledge base and value system.
4. The information literate student, individually or as a member of a group, uses information effectively to accomplish a specific purpose.
5. The information literate student understands many of the economic, legal, and social issues surrounding the use of information and accesses and uses information ethically and legally.

www.ala.org/ala/mgrps/divs/acrl/standards/informationliteracycompetency.cfm

Summary

Embedded librarianship means getting into the LMS, gaining access to a course's classroom or site, and offering assistance to students. It has been established as a library service for at least 10 years, and its non-LMS antecedents for much longer. LMS embedded librarians work at institutions of varying size and academic levels and offer a diverse palette of services.

LMS embedded librarianship pairs especially well with online and hybrid learning and provides equitable access to library resources and services. Online learning continues to grow; enrollment will reach nearly four million students by 2014 (Online Learning 2010). These faculty and students have seen the new information landscape and have ratcheted up their research expectations. LMS embedded librarianship delivers what they seek.

Students benefit from working with LMS embedded librarians who will introduce them to scholarly research resources and methods. It is incumbent upon librarians to join students in the LMS by collaborating with faculty to provide information literacy instruction as needed and to market the abundance of the academic library's collection. The tools of scholarly research continue to change and users must be kept apprised by librarians while organizations like the American

Library Association continue to discuss the core standards of information literacy needed by all to participate and be productive in the information world.

References

Armstrong, Annie. 2012. "Marketing the Library's Instructional Services to Teaching Faculty: Learning from Teaching Faculty Interviews." In *College Libraries and Student Culture: What We Now Know,* edited by Lynda M. Duke and Andrew D. Asher, 31–48. Chicago: American Library Association.

Asher, Andrew D., and Lynda M. Duke. 2012a. "Conclusion and Future Research." In *College Libraries and Student Culture: What We Now Know,* edited by Lynda M. Duke and Andrew D. Asher, 161–167. Chicago: American Library Association.

Asher, Andrew D., and Lynda M. Duke. 2012b. "Searching for Answers: Student Research Behavior at Illinois Wesleyan University." In *College Libraries and Student Culture: What We Now Know,* edited by Lynda M. Duke and Andrew D. Asher, 71–86. Chicago: American Library Association.

Association of College and Research Libraries. 2000. "Information Literacy CompetencyStandards for Higher Education." www.ala.org/ala/mgrps/divs/acrl/standards/informationliteracycompetency.cfm.

Bauwens, Michel. 1993. "The Cybrarians Manifesto." *Business Information Review* 9 (4): 65–67.

Bell, Steven J. 2009. "The Library Web Site of the Future?" *Inside Higher Education* (blog). February 17. www.insidehighered.com/views/2009/02/17/bell.

Cox, Christopher. 2002. "Becoming Part of the Course." *College and Research Libraries News* 63 (1): 11.

Davenport, Tom, and Larry Prusak. 1993. "Blow Up the Corporate Library." *International Journal of Information Management* 13: 405–412.

Dewey, Barbara I. 2004. "The Embedded Librarian: Strategic Campus Collaborations." *Resource Sharing and Information Networks* 17 (1/2): 5–17.

Dorner, Jennifer L., Susan E. Taylor, and Kay Hodson-Carlton. 2001. "Faculty-Librarian Collaboration for Nursing Information Literacy: A Tiered Approach." *Reference Services Review* 29 (2): 132–140.

Drewes, Kathy, and Nadine Hoffman. 2010. "Academic Embedded Librarianship: An Introduction." *Public Services Quarterly* 6 (2/3): 75–82.

Duke, Lynda M., and Andrew D. Asher, eds. 2012. *College Libraries and Student Culture: What We Now Know.* Chicago: American Library Association.

Head, Alison J., and Michael B. Eisenberg. 2009. "Lessons Learned: How College Students Seek Information in the Digital Age." Project Information Literacy First Year Report with Student Survey Findings, University of Washington's Information School. http://projectinfolit.org/pdfs/PIL_Fall2009_finalv_YR1_12_2009v2.pdf.

Head, Alison J., and Michael B. Eisenberg. 2010a. "Assigning Inquiry: How Handouts for Research Assignments Guide Today's College Students." Project Information Literacy Progress Report, University of Washington's Information School. July 13. http://projectinfolit.org/pdfs/PIL_Handout_Study_finalvJuly_2010.pdf.

Head, Alison J., and Michael B. Eisenberg. 2010b. "Truth Be Told: How College Students Evaluate and Use Information in the Digital Age." Project Information Literacy Progress Report, University of Washington's Information School. http://projectinfolit.org/pdfs/PIL_Fall2010_Survey_FullReport1.pdf.

Head, Alison J., and Michael B. Eisenberg. 2011. "College Students Eager To Learn But Need Help Negotiating Information Overload." *Seattle Times,* June 3. http://seattletimes.com/html/opinion/2015227485_guest05head.html.

Kesselman, Martin A., and Sarah Barbara Watstein. 2009. "Creating Opportunities: Embedded Librarians." *Journal of Library Administration* 49 (4): 383–400. *Academic Search Complete,* EBSCO*host.*

Kolowich, Steve. 2011. "What Students Don't Know." *Inside Higher Ed,* August 22. www.insidehighered.com/layout/set/print/news/2011/08/22/erial.

Lipscomb, Carolyn E. 2000. "Clinical Librarianship." *Bulletin of the Medical Library Association* 88 (4): 393–396.

Miller, Susan, and Nancy Murillo. 2012. "Why Don't Students Ask Librarians for Help?: Undergraduate Help-Seeking Behavior in Three Academic Libraries." In *College Libraries and Student Culture: What We Now Know,* edited by Lynda M. Duke and Andrew D. Asher, 49–70. Chicago: American Library Association.

Oder, Norman, and Lynn Blumenstein. 2010. "Personal Librarian Program at Drexel University." *Library Journal* 135 (16): 14. *Library,*

Information Science and Technology Abstracts with Full Text, EBSCO*host.*

OCLC. 2011. "The Library Brand 2010." *OCLC Perceptions of Libraries, 2010: Context and Community. Dublin, OH: OCLC.* www.oclc.org/reports/2010perceptions/2010perceptions_all.pdf.

"Online Learning: By the Numbers." *Chronicle of Higher Education* 57 (11): B28-B29.

Shumaker, David, and Laura Ann Tyler. 2007. "Embedded Library Services: An Initial Inquiry Into Practices for Their Development, Management, and Delivery." Paper presented at Special Libraries Association Annual Conference, Denver, CO, June 6. www.sla.org/pdfs/sla2007/ShumakerEmbeddedLibSvcs.pdf.

"Team Teaching with an Embedded Librarian." 2008. *Distance Education Report* 12 (17): 6–7.

Thomsett-Scott, Beth, and Patricia E. Reese. 2006. "Changes in Library Technology and Reference Desk Statistics: Is There a Relationship?" *Public Services Quarterly* 2 (2/)3: 143–165.

Yarmey-Tylutki, Kristen. 2010. "When Students Go Mobile." *Pennsylvania Library Association Bulletin* 65 (4): 13–15.

The Embedded Librarian and the LMS

The LMS has emerged as a web-based component to support teaching and learning. Though present in K-12 education and in both corporate and not-for-profit training environments, the LMS has become a key facet of higher education. In a world of ever-present connections, having a digital location for sharing course documents, engaging in synchronous and asynchronous communication, and collaborating on assignments are necessities. A given college or university may have one or more LMSs in place, depending on local needs and technology policies. This chapter will describe this nexus of academic work, investigate how librarians have become integrated within it, and suggest methods for the new embedded librarian to, well, *become embedded.*

IN THIS CHAPTER:

Why the LMS?

The LMS as a general concept meets various needs in higher education. Some of these needs are suggested by the names used to refer to these systems collectively (see the sidebar). Of these, LMS is the most widely-used acronym (and the one chosen for this book), though VLE and MLE are the preferred terms within the United Kingdom and Europe. CLE is being advanced as an acronym by users of Sakai, because it stresses the collaborative nature of group assignments and the shared creation methods (such as using a wiki) that can be used in an LMS. The oft-repeated terms in these names are "management" and "learning," which might suggest an oxymoron—can the learning process of a set of individuals be managed?

Many names for the LMS

- CLE–Collaboration and Learning Environment
- CMS–Course Management System
- LMS–Learning Management System
- MLE–Managed Learning Environment
- VLE–Virtual Learning Environment

Calling an LMS a management tool may be an overstatement, but it does give instructors tools for organizing class activities, sharing documents, administering tests and quizzes, communicating with students, and providing grades and feedback. These tools can be readily directed toward one group of students at a time through the LMS in a classroom or course site (multiple sections of the same course can also be combined into one classroom or course site). Copyrighted resources can be shared with just the students in an individual class, in keeping with copyright provisions and online course guidelines (discussed further in chapter 6). Grades can be transmitted from the individual course site into the college or university's grading and registration management software (e.g., Banner, Oracle, Jenzabar, Campus Management). University-wide messages, calendars, and other information can be shared with all classes at once. This combination of focus on a given course (and class) and integration with other institutional management capacities makes the LMS an excellent vehicle for course materials and interactions.

Nearly all colleges and universities have an LMS in place, whether commercial, open source, or homegrown in nature. Usage across courses and disciplines varies from institution to institution, with some showing broad adoption of the LMS by faculty members and others revealing pockets of intense usage among certain departments or in certain types of courses. The 2011 Campus Computing Survey found that 59 percent of all courses use the LMS, with 67 percent of public university courses utilizing the LMS and 51 percent of community college courses doing the same (Campus Computing Project 2011). A recent EDUCAUSE survey found that 73 percent of undergraduate students use an LMS and 27 percent use it multiple times per day (Dahlstrom et al. 2011). While the range of aspects and tools make the LMS suited for completely online courses, it is also used widely as an online supplement for face-to-face courses. Instructors may also utilize the LMS to combine these two course models in a hybrid course, spending some portion of the class online and the rest in the classroom.

LMS Choices

The LMS market in higher education, much like the integrated library systems market, has been characterized by many mergers and the subsequent disappearance of competing products. A review of the major products in place shows one dominant player and three solid performers. Blackboard (see figure 2.1) has remained the comfortable leader by buying up its competitors WebCT and ANGEL, but has dropped its market share from 71 percent in 2006 to 51 percent in 2011 (Campus Computing Project 2011). That earlier pair of mergers left Desire2Learn as the only privately-held competitor to Blackboard on the market. Other alternatives include the open-source products Moodle (see figure 2.2) and Sakai (see figure 2.3), which each hold significant and growing portions of the market. A chart created by Phil Hill (found at www.deltainitiative.com/index.php/phils-blog/70-new-mentality-enters-lms-market) offers a useful way to view the history of developments among different LMSs (Hill 2011). It illustrates LMS products (and their subsequent name changes and mergers) from 1996 to the present.

The authors' survey of embedded librarians (see the appendix) included the question, "Which LMS are you using (or have you used) with embedded courses at your institution?" The market share of systems among embedded librarian institutions tracks very well with the results of the nationwide survey in the sidebar. The list below shows the number of respondents who chose each response and their percentage of the 280 total respondents (respondents were encouraged to mark all applicable responses):

- Blackboard (145)—56 percent
- Moodle (43)—16 percent
- ANGEL (36)—14 percent
- Desire2Learn (26)—10 percent
- WebCT (24)—9 percent
- Sakai (18)—7 percent
- Other (31)—12 percent

A new competitor in the LMS market is Pearson, an academic publisher, which announced in late 2011 that it would develop a freely available LMS called OpenClass. Pearson's partner in the effort is Google, which has created much expectation and speculation about the introduction of OpenClass. Can Google's wide reach, product development prowess, and name recognition help Pearson break into the LMS market? Will OpenClass be a success, like Google Docs, or more of a momentary blip, like Google Buzz? These questions will be answered in 2013, but given Google's track record there is a solid

Market Share of Higher Education Institutions Reporting a Single, Standard LMS

- Blackboard–51 percent
- Moodle–19 percent
- Desire2Learn–11 percent
- Sakai–7 percent
- Jenzabar–2 percent
- Other–2 percent
- eCollege–1 percent
- Instructure–1 percent
- No standard LMS–7 percent

(Taken from the Campus Computing Project's Campus Computing Survey 2011)

FIGURE 2.1 Screenshot of Blackboard Classroom

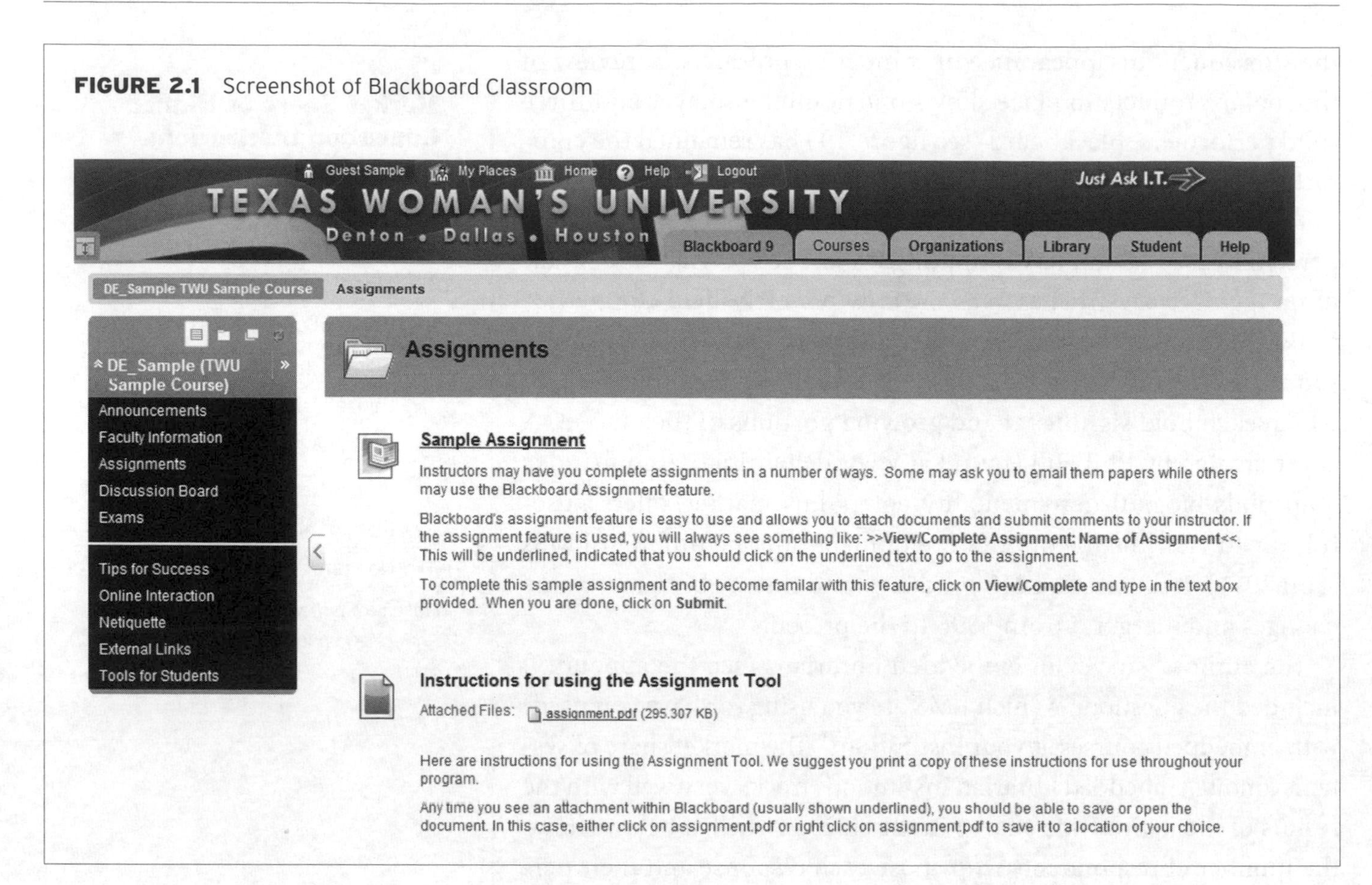

chance that OpenClass could become an appealing new LMS option for academic users.

Common Features and Tools among the LMSs

Though the systems differ in aesthetics and programming, there are common tasks and characteristics that an embedded librarian can use in any LMS. Below is an annotated list of tools that have particular interest for librarians, though it should not limit anyone's imagination for finding ways to engage with students in their class work. A wider list of LMS features can be viewed at the WCET EduTools CMS comparison site (www.edutools.info/static.jsp?pj=4&page=HOME).

This chapter is not meant to be a buying guide for LMS nor cover all features that may be of interest. The WCET site can serve that

FIGURE 2.2 Screenshot of Moodle Course

moodle.org moodle.com

Higher Education Film Studies Module

Home ◻ Courses ◻ English ◻ Film Studies ◻ General ◻ Course Overview and Approach

Course Overview

This course will run on a themed basis, taking approximate times for each section or block of material (outlined at the end of each block). You are welcome to jump to sections that interest you more than others but, in the interest of building an online learning community that is communicative, you are asked to do your best to keep up with the readings and activities as they are active. You will get more out of this course if you feel you can offer your opinions and ideas in activities and expect to get a response from your classmates because they too are working on the same material. Each section follows a linear pattern, however, again, please feel free to adjust your learning to your own preferred style; in other words, if you prefer to watch the films before doing the readings or vice versa, please do so.

Approach: Interaction and Communication

As the most significant portion of the course is delivered online, you will be directed to specific threads in forum discussions and asked to answer questions, to offer your views and, generally, to contribute to discussions on a variety of topics. Additionally, you will be expected to keep an online journal of your own perceptions of both the course material and your changing ideas and views on notions of culture and technology as the course progresses, as well as to continually challenge your own definitions of terms in the online course Glossaries. **Note: Instructions on journal and glossary activities will be clearly given at specific times throughout the course. Should you have any questions regarding this, please do not hesitate to post a note in the** Help Forum.

This is a highly interactive course that offers students the opportunity to exchange ideas as well as to discuss and collaborate on notions of gender, technology and culture.

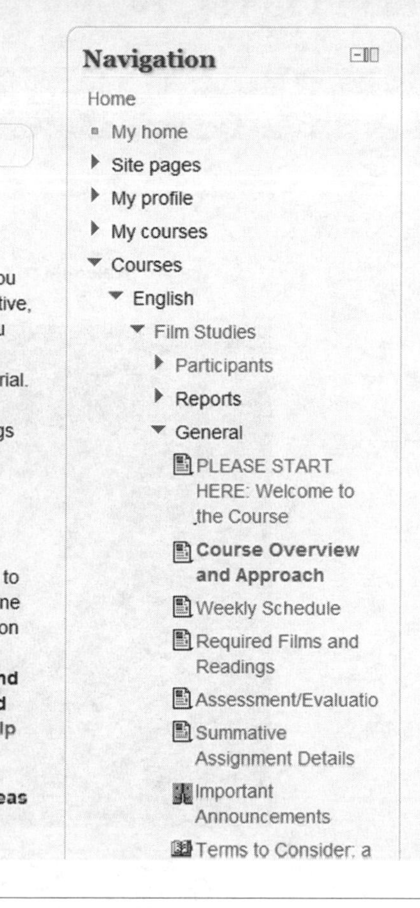

purpose by providing detailed overviews of several products, including comparisons of up to 10 LMSs simultaneously.

Posting Content

All of the current LMS products provide methods for posting content related to a given course. This content can be narrative text and images describing course content, lecture slides or outlines, assignment directions, and so forth (figure 2.5). Instructors can create and edit documents within the LMS, even pasting in text and images from files created elsewhere, so that the resulting combination of text and images appears right within the course pages. They can also attach files in various formats that are then stored within the LMS for students to access in their classroom or course site. Students open the

FIGURE 2.3 Screenshot of Sakai Course Site

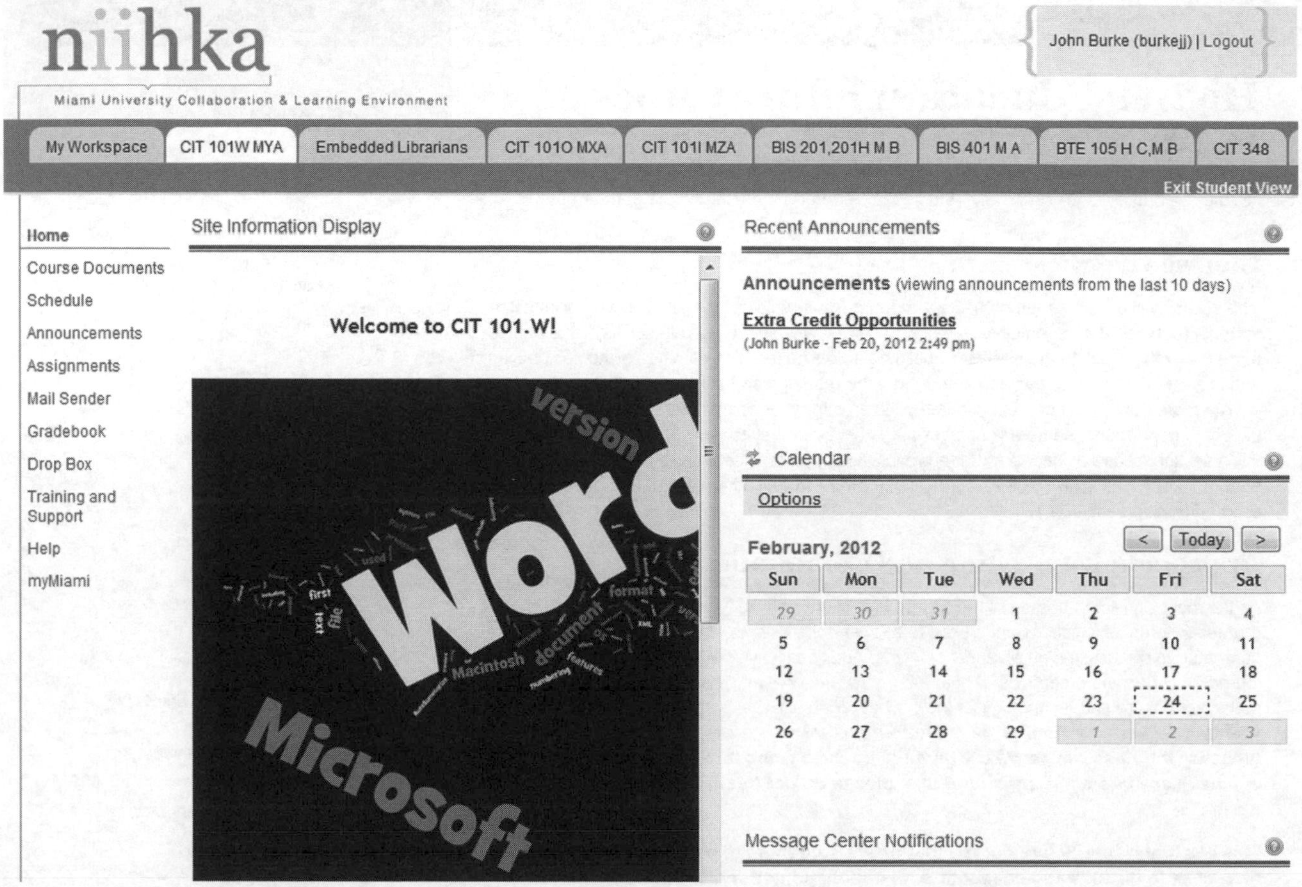

files using third-party applications like Adobe Acrobat Reader or Microsoft Word, or use their web browser to view and make use of the information. Instructors may also choose to add links to web-based content by entering URLs and short descriptions in a list or within a lesson or module they create. This capacity allows for a flexible amount of material, authored by the faculty member or by others, to be placed in or linked from the classroom.

E-mailing Students

E-mail is a regular method of communication within the LMS through which the instructor and class members can quickly connect with one another. It is generally a tool that is used for sending e-mail from within the LMS interface to individual students' e-mail

FIGURE 2.4 Screenshot of Desire2Learn Course

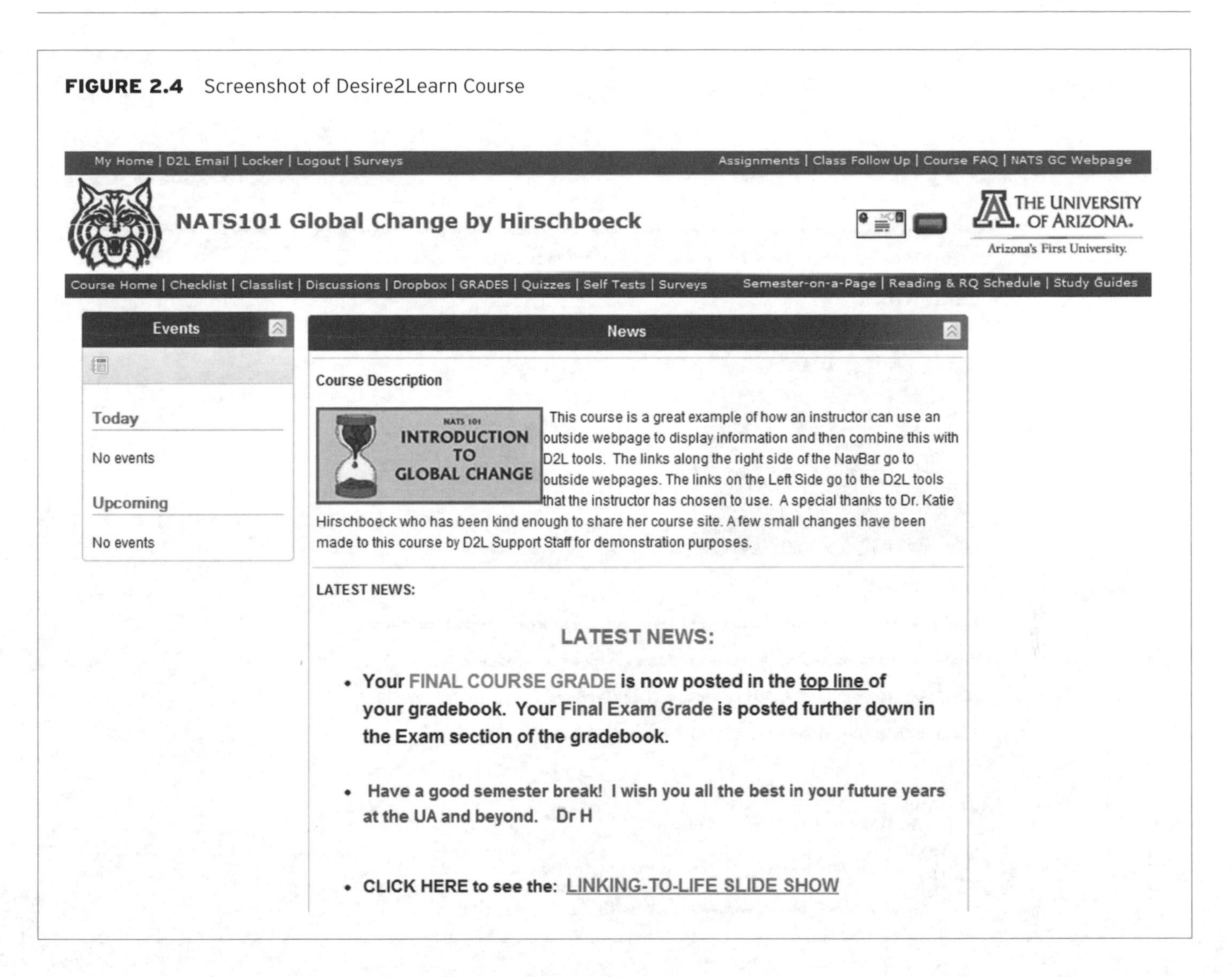

accounts, not as a means for faculty and students to read their mail within the interface. The general idea is that the LMS can quickly provide the e-mail addresses for members of the class, making it a matter of a few clicks to e-mail everyone without having to type individual e-mail addresses. Instructors can send quick updates on class schedule changes or reminders of upcoming assignments or course tasks. It is also handy for students to use when contacting the members of a project or study group, or to locate their instructor's e-mail for direct communication. Moodle uses its Forum tool to accomplish this purpose (see figure 2.6), Blackboard and Desire-2Learn (see figure 2.4) have an e-mail application, and Sakai has its Mailtool. Some LMS tools (beyond the e-mail application) can also be set to automatically e-mail students when new assignments are posted or when grades have been released.

FIGURE 2.5 Screenshot of Content Display From an LMS

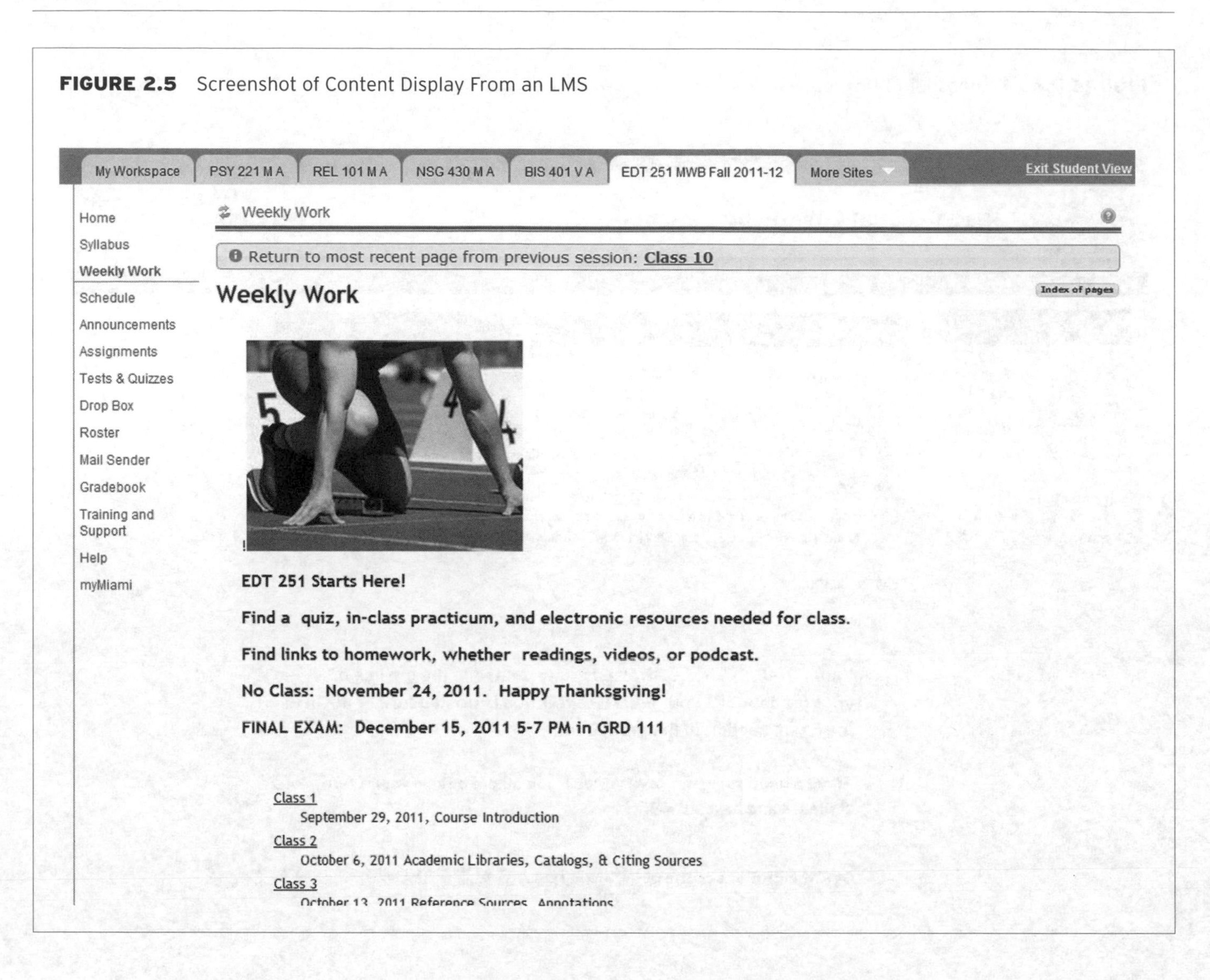

Discussion Boards or Forums

Discussion boards and forums provide opportunities within the LMS for structured discussions on class topics. Instructors can establish individual forums for course topics, weekly discussions, or whatever they deem necessary. They can then post questions or topics within each forum that students can respond to with their own posts. Some instructors may use a single forum for both general questions and ongoing discussion assignments. The boards or forums allow for interactive discussions between instructor and student and also among students responding to one another's posts. They also provide a transcript of information related to course topics that students can review. Instructors tend to use them as an alternative to having students keep written journals on course readings or other materials.

FIGURE 2.6 Screenshot of Forum Tool

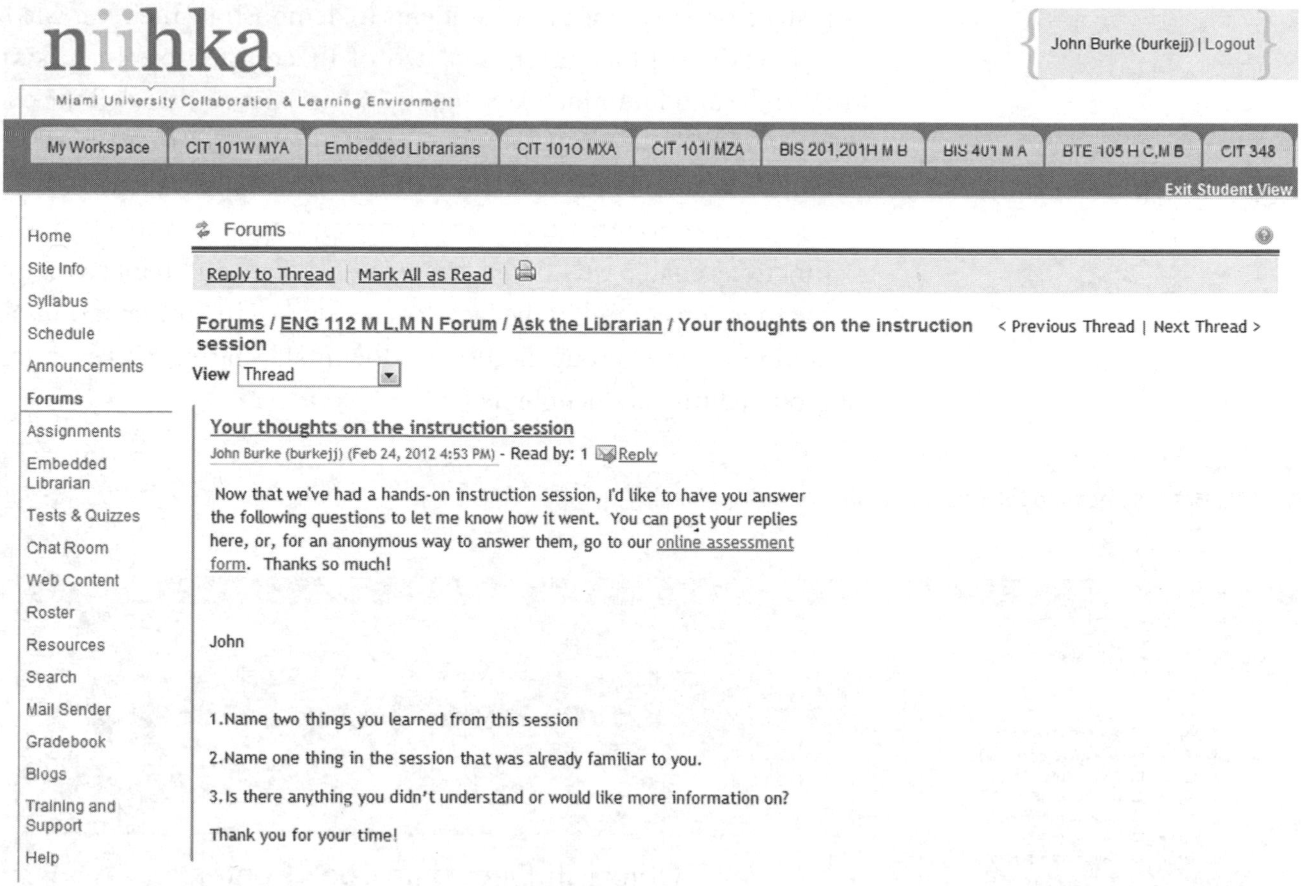

niihka
Miami University Collaboration & Learning Environment
John Burke (burkejj) | Logout
My Workspace | CIT 101W MYA | Embedded Librarians | CIT 101O MXA | CIT 101I MZA | BIS 201,201H M B | BIS 401 M A | BTE 105 H C,M B | CIT 348
Exit Student View
Home
Site Info
Syllabus
Schedule
Announcements
Forums
Assignments
Embedded Librarian
Tests & Quizzes
Chat Room
Web Content
Roster
Resources
Search
Mail Sender
Gradebook
Blogs
Training and Support
Help
Forums
Reply to Thread | Mark All as Read
Forums / ENG 112 M L,M N Forum / Ask the Librarian / Your thoughts on the instruction session
< Previous Thread | Next Thread >
View Thread
Your thoughts on the instruction session
John Burke (burkejj) (Feb 24, 2012 4:53 PM) - Read by: 1 Reply
Now that we've had a hands-on instruction session, I'd like to have you answer the following questions to let me know how it went. You can post your replies here, or, for an anonymous way to answer them, go to our online assessment form. Thanks so much!
John
1.Name two things you learned from this session
2.Name one thing in the session that was already familiar to you.
3.Is there anything you didn't understand or would like more information on?
Thank you for your time!

They are also meant to encourage interaction among students as they explore class topics. Blackboard has discussion boards, Moodle and Sakai have forums, and Desire2Learn has a discussions tool.

Synchronous Chat/Web Conferencing and Collaboration

In addition to the asynchronous communication methods listed above, each LMS has the means of bringing the class and instructor together for synchronous interactions. At a minimum, this interaction involves text-only chat between participants to allow a real-time sharing of questions and class information. There are third-party tools that can be added onto the features of the LMS to provide a shared whiteboard experience that allows video, audio, and web browsing to be shared among the participants. This combination lets participants use a greater diversity of materials and to be flexible about how they can ask and answer questions. Drawing out a diagram or an equation on a whiteboard can be a powerful way to teach a concept as an instructor or as a means for students to demonstrate their knowledge.

Blackboard has purchased two of its competitors in this area (Wimba and Elluminate, see figure 2.7) and has re-branded the combination of these new tools and its own in-house tool for collaboration as Blackboard Collaborate. It will be available to Blackboard customers as well as to other LMSs as a free-standing tool. Altogether, these functions enable web-based classes to simulate and replace many of the functions found in the face-to-face classroom: presentations and demonstrations, group discussion, document sharing, and even some group editing of documents.

FIGURE 2.7 Screenshot of Elluminate Session

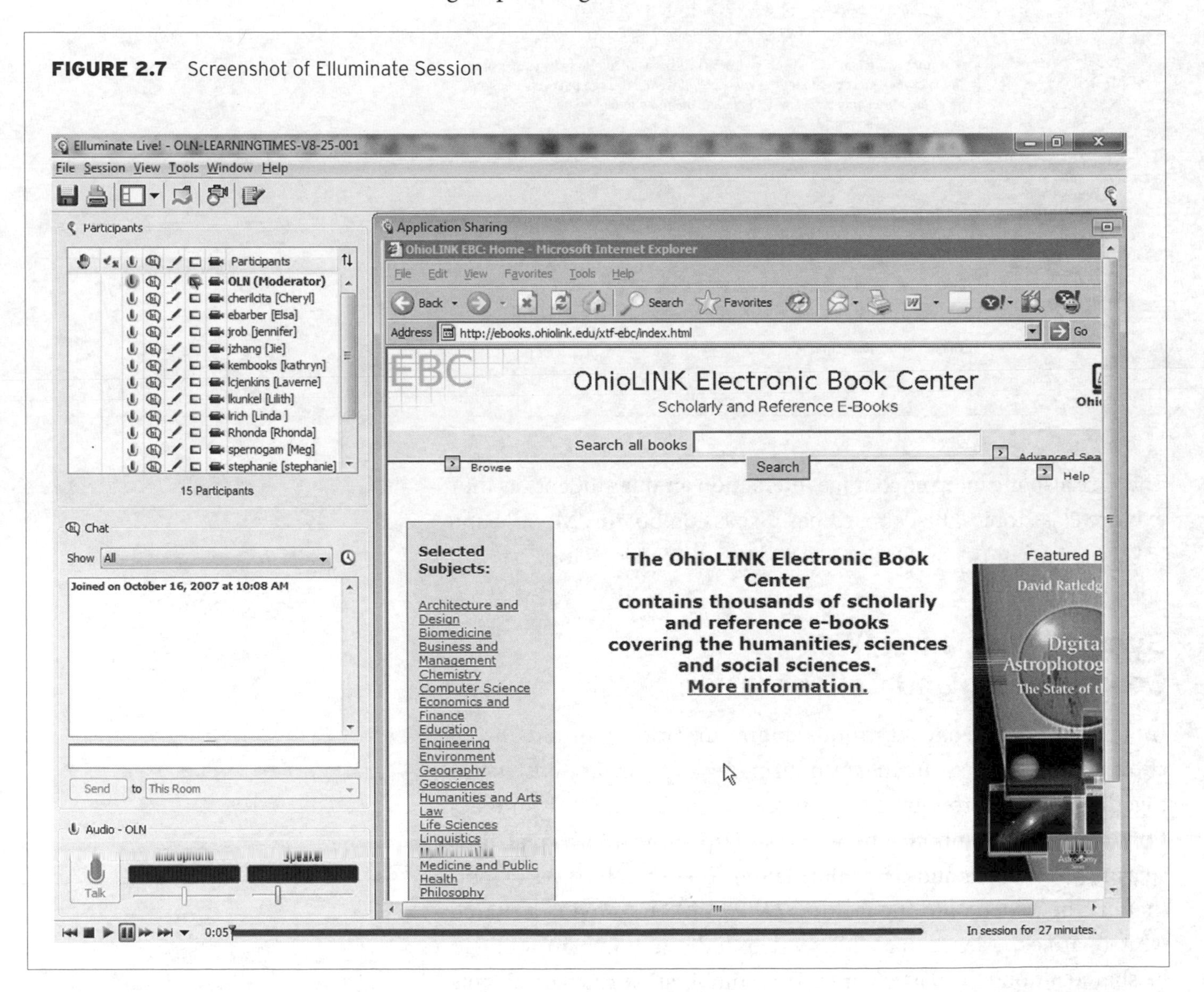

What Information and Resources Could Librarians Share in the LMS?

How then can embedded librarians best utilize the information sharing methods in the LMS to teach information literacy skills and provide reference and other library services? Here are some possible ways that an embedded librarian can incorporate library information and resources into the LMS:

- Links to library databases and other resources can be posted within the course. This can be done in a contained space dedicated to the embedded librarian, a single page of linked documents in the course site, or it can be done in a more piecemeal fashion, mixed in with other course content. Links can be made to the library website, LibGuides or other subject-related course guides created by librarians, to freely available websites, or to individual databases or other subscription resources. This can bring those resources right into the classroom, putting them as close as possible to where students may need them.
- Information on research concepts can be placed in a similar fashion. Brief explanations of key information literacy topics can be included in the course site for student's review. Topics might include distinguishing between scholarly and popular periodical articles, choosing or narrowing research topics, avoiding plagiarism, citing sources properly within the required citation style, or understanding the merits of different types of information sources (articles, books, websites, etc.). These elements of many library instruction sessions and reference interactions are also necessary in the embedded context, and have the opportunity there to be viewed and reviewed by students.
- Suggested research strategies for course assignments can also be included, and are perhaps best placed alongside the assignment in question. The librarian can offer pertinent advice to students on approaching the assignment and gathering needed information. This might involve a set of step-by-step instructions on moving from resource to resource, or suggestions on narrowing options to use in individual databases, or tips on approaching a set of resources and

choosing the ones that might best fit their topic. As well, any material that might be placed in a handout for classes or given verbally to students can be captured and offered in the course site. The flexibility of the LMS for posting documents or other files can lead a librarian to create screenshots to accompany the suggested steps and help clarify them. Moderation is called for, but again there is great opportunity for suggestions to be reviewed in the LMS, rather than forgotten or discarded.

- Tutorials on using databases or planning searches can be useful additions to a course site. These items may encompass some of the materials noted above, but they are worthy of special note. Tutorials, whether embedded in the course site so that they can be watched without leaving the page, or linked from YouTube or the library website, bring a method of visually communicating important

FIGURE 2.8 Screenshot of Embedded Librarian Contact Information and Chat Widget

The Embedded Librarian: Your Guide to Finding the Information You Need

Hello! I'm John Burke and I'm your librarian. My job is to help you find the information you need for your assignments in BIS 201.

If you have a question about where to look for articles, books, web sites, or other information, how to find scholarly information, how to cite sources in your bibliography, or anything else, please feel free to contact me at burkejj@muohio.edu or 513-727-3293. You may also IM me at **infomanjjb** on Meebo or AIM, or IM our staff member on duty by using the widget on the right or on our library web site. Don't forget our handy text help service: just text your questions to 513-393-9141.

You may also use our Research Consultation form to make an appointment with me or any of our librarians.

I'm generally in the library from 8-5, Monday through Friday (my office is behind the InfoDesk). I check my email anytime I'm awake, so you can nearly always get an answer from me fairly quickly.

What's all this about peer-reviewed articles

Click to learn about

Peer Review in Five Minutes

elements of library information. Examples might include a step-by-step screencast of navigating and searching a database, a video tour of the library, or interesting case examples of a student doing the same research that the class is about to embark on.

- A key piece of information to include in the embedded course is contact information for the embedded librarian (see figure 2.8). Students should be encouraged to follow up with the embedded librarian when they have questions or run into research roadblocks. Contact information can include the plain text of names, e-mail addresses, and phone numbers, or can be expanded to include active IM/chat/texting widgets for the librarian's personal account or a regularly staffed library-wide account. Librarians may also provide links or information on the library's open hours or the hours when they or other reference staff members are available. The main idea is to make help available to students when they need it.

What Could Librarians Communicate with LMS Tools?

As defined above, the LMS offers methods for both synchronous and asynchronous communication that embedded librarians may also use. Strategic methods for doing so would include the following:

- Aside from the ability to copy the address or click a link to e-mail the embedded librarian from a separate e-mail application, students can also see the librarian listed in the LMS e-mail application. This link may be categorized under instructors, teaching assistants, or elsewhere, depending on the status of the librarian within the course. In any event, by participating in the course the librarian can provide students an easy way to reach a librarian by e-mail. The librarian can also receive e-mails related to the class that are sent to all participants. This can alert librarians to developments in the class that the instructor e-mails about, but also to questions that students ask related to course content or assignments. The judicious embedded librarian can choose opportunities to insert relevant information into replies to questions meant for the instructor or the class as a whole.

- Regularly monitoring the discussion board or forum in a course site provides the embedded librarian with similar opportunities to share helpful information. The structure of a given course might mean that there are certain opportune times to scan student postings for questions related to information-gathering assignments. Depending on the time available to the librarian, it may also make sense to regularly venture into the discussion board or forum to stay aware of course developments and catch unexpected questions or comments and share information. Another model to follow is to establish a forum or ongoing discussion topic where students can post questions directly for the librarian.
- On the synchronous side of communications, the embedded librarian can utilize collaboration tools for multiple types of interactions. The whole class or groups working on projects could utilize established chat reference hours to consult with the librarian. The librarian could provide full instruction sessions to the class, demonstrating databases and the library website through shared browsing. The collaboration tool can be used as a regular piece of each semester's services to embedded classes, or as a just-in-time tool to meet an unexpected course need for guidance. The option of being able to work interactively with a student or students who cannot walk into the library has multiple possibilities.

Examples of Embedded Librarians in the LMS

So what do these combinations of tools and purposes look like in actual courses with embedded librarians? Below are three examples of librarians implementing these options in four different LMSs: Blackboard, Desire2Learn, Sakai, and Moodle.

Northern Kentucky University—Blackboard

At Northern Kentucky University, an embedded librarian program was started in the university's Blackboard LMS in 2007. A key element of the program was the creation of a shared collection of library instruction resources (handouts, tutorials, resource lists) created jointly by members of the reference and instructional staff. The collection was housed in a community site within Blackboard, making it easy for embedded librarians to access and move content into their respective course classrooms. In addition to having elements of this collection posted in individual classrooms, embedded librarians communicate with students through the discussion board. This allows them to answer general student questions about research and also to highlight specific databases and search strategies. One other element of their use of the discussion board is that students are encouraged to place specific reference questions on it, with the guarantee that their embedded librarian will answer it by a specified time. This has had two benefits: first, that all students in the class will see the answer from the librarian and will learn something that they may well have asked about separately, and second, that moving much reference question activity into the LMS has allowed librarians to reduce staffing hours at the library's reference desk. The library now sees embedded librarianship evolving as its main method of delivering library service (Chesnut 2010).

East Tennessee State University—Desire2Learn

In an effort to reach across subject disciplines and provide library instruction to the vast majority of students, East Tennessee University distributed an instructional module through its LMS. While the library staff had created LibGuides to cover subject-specific resources and connect students with subject liaisons, they did not have a way of delivering more foundational library information. A shortage of librarians and the immense amount of time required to reach classes synchronously made face-to-face instruction impossible. The librarians created a module in Desire2Learn that could be placed in any course. The module included videos, documents, and links to databases and library website content (links to citation tools, etc.) meant to address eight different topics. A quiz was also created as part of the module that could be used by faculty as a way of assessing students' learning from the materials (Adebonojo 2011).

The Community College of Vermont—Moodle

At the Community College of Vermont, the forum is the focus of embedded librarian efforts. A forum is provided in embedded librarian classes to answer questions from students. Librarians provide focused threads during the course, posting a welcome and contact information, followed by research strategies, how to find class-related journals, how to use databases and the library website, and so forth. Posted material consists of narrative text, embedded tutorials, and lists of links. Thanks to the archived nature of the forum in Moodle (as in other LMSs), students can return to previously posted materials, and can also learn from questions posted by other students. The forum may be very active for a given class, and the librarians encourage faculty to monitor it as well to provide content- or assignment-specific input (Hartness Library 2012).

Miami University Middletown—Sakai

At the Middletown regional campus of Miami University, embedded librarians have utilized both Blackboard and Sakai. Starting in 2008, librarians began placing links to course-related databases and librarian contact information in the LMS. This expanded with the addition of video tutorials and searching tips in subsequent years, along with participating in course discussion boards and sending e-mails to students. Contact with students has increased over the years, with students dropping into the library for research consultations or connecting with their embedded librarian through e-mail and instant messaging. In several courses, embedded librarians have been able to place resource links or advice to students next to or in the same document as the faculty member's assignment. In 2011, the university transitioned to a new institution-wide LMS, moving from Blackboard to Sakai in less than a year. The librarians overcame the same obstacles and adjustments that faculty faced with the move, even serving on the Sakai training team to assist faculty. The new LMS provided new possibilities for connecting with students, but many of the tools were similar and allowed for a relatively quick initial transition. Now moving into their second semester with Sakai, the librarians are looking for new elements of the LMS to use, going beyond the creation of an embedded librarian document and using the Forum and Mailtool.

Questions to Consider When Implementing Embedded Librarianship in the LMS

There are a few final items to consider when embedding in the LMS at a given institution. First of all, does the institution use a single, standard LMS, or are there multiple products in place? While the most common situation is to have only one LMS, the Campus Computing Project (2011) notes that 7 percent of reporting institutions have no standard in place. In addition to this, there may well be situations in which a campus has a standard LMS, but there are still individual colleges or schools within the institution that use a separate LMS. This issue becomes important to the prospective embedded librarian in that it is easier to work within a single LMS environment. Librarians do not need to learn multiple systems or adapt content to fit the rules of separate systems. It is not an intractable problem to have multiple LMSs in place, but it is good to know whether it will be necessary to work around this.

The next question is what status options or roles an LMS provides for users, and how differences in these status choices may affect the work of embedded librarians. For instance, in Blackboard a user can be classified as a student, faculty member, or a course builder. The course builder can add materials to the course classroom and remove them as needed, but is unable to see the course grade book or to access course usage statistics. In Sakai, there is a teaching assistant status (in addition to students and faculty) that allows access to course content and the grade book, but does not automatically give permission to edit content. Moodle has some standard roles set in addition to teacher and student, including one for course creator that allows for content addition to the course. Desire2Learn has a similar arrangement to the others, and all of the systems allow for custom roles to be created that fit the needs of the local implementation. The key element is that librarians need to know what status or role options are available and what permissions each of these roles and statuses have. In some cases, a non-instructor role may work well for adding content and communicating within the course, while in others it will be easiest and more effective to give librarians a faculty or instructor role.

Finally, are instruction librarians already familiar with the LMS or will working with the system be a new experience? Prospective embedded librarians should take advantage of institution-provided training or documentation to acquaint themselves with the LMS and to learn specific tasks. Librarians may have already established organizational sites or in-house training sites using the LMS. In some situations, librarians may have had adjunct faculty roles at the institution in which they used the LMS with a class. All LMS products have the ability to create practice courses or sites within them, which is highly recommended for librarians who are preparing an embedded program to learn to navigate the system and practice activities.

Summary

The LMS is a very commonly used tool within higher education. LMS options continue to evolve, but Blackboard, Moodle, Desire2Learn, and Sakai hold the largest market shares. Librarians can make use of various tools within the LMS to post searching information, link to resources, and to communicate with students. Chapter 5 will provide more guidance on how to design and create instructional tools.

References

Adebonojo, Leslie G. 2011. "A Way to Reach All of Your Students: The Course Management System." *Journal of Library and Information Services in Distance Learning* 5: 105–113.

Campus Computing Project. 2011. "2011 National Survey of Information Technology in U.S. Higher Education." www.campuscomputing.net/sites/www.campuscomputing.net/files/Green-CampusComputing2011_2.pdf.

Chesnut, Mary Todd, Threasa L. Wesley, and Robert Zai. 2010. "Adding an Extra Helping of Service When You Already Have a Full Plate: Building an Embedded Librarian Program." *Public Services Quarterly* 6 (2/3): 122–129.

Dahlstrom, Eden, Tom de Boor, Peter Grunwald, and Martha Vockley. 2011. "The ECAR National Study of Undergraduate Students and Information Technology, 2011 (Research Report)." EDUCAUSE Center for Applied Research. www.educause.edu/ecar.

EduTools. 2011. "CMS: CMS Product List." WCET EduTools. www.edutools.info/static.jsp?pj=4&page=HOME.

Hartness Library. 2012. "CCV's Embedded Librarian Program." http://youtu.be/NZqI1b2bJcI.

Hill, Phil. 2011. "New Mentality Enters LMS Market." *Delta Initiative.* www.deltainitiative.com/index.php/phils-blog/70-new-mentality-enters-lms-market.

Creating a Pilot Program

> In the fall semester 2007, as interest in the early experiments with embedded librarians service developed, questions about the feasibility of adding one more service to an already full and highly utilized suite of reference and instructional services inevitably entered our [Northern Kentucky University's W. Frank Steely Library] discussion. (Chesnut, Wesley, and Zai 2010, 122)

IN THIS CHAPTER:

- ✓ Scope of a Pilot Program
- ✓ Planning a Pilot Program
- ✓ Becoming Informed about Programs and Best Practices
- ✓ Building Skills with the LMS
- ✓ Selecting Services to Offer
- ✓ Identifying and Recruiting Faculty Collaborators
- ✓ Implementing the Pilot
- ✓ Assessing the Results
- ✓ Modifying and Improving
- ✓ Summary
- ✓ References

Scope of a Pilot Program

By definition a pilot is a small-scale trial which is run to discover and correct potential problems before undertaking a full-scale program. It minimizes the risks, errors, and costs associated with offering a new service or program. Pilots are not about perfection; rather, they foster experimentation. An overworked but proactive librarian might muse, "Can we do it, should we do it?" The preceding quotation from Northern Kentucky University's Steely Library illustrates this point. A pilot was conducted there which confirmed the significance of the program and was to alter their existing service model.

An LMS embedded librarianship pilot need only involve a few faculty members, but how few? One or two faculty members with whom a librarian has already established a working relationship may be ideal. A pilot might also be run involving faculty from a single department, such as nursing, for which one serves as departmental liaison. A pilot's membership might be comprised of faculty within a given program, such as online learning. On a smaller campus, a pilot might be run for a predetermined number of volunteer instructors, limited perhaps by equipment requirements, funds, or number of librarians.

At Duke University, four librarians ran a Blackboard pilot with 12 faculty in the fall of 2007 (Daly 2010). In the case of Valdosta State University, its LMS embedded librarians planned to run a pilot in the summer of 2011 by inviting all faculty to a drop-in informational session about the two models of embedded librarianship available, with the hope of serving the information literacy needs of distance and online students (Wright and Williams 2011). In contrast, at The George Washington University's Himmelfarb Health Sciences Library, one proactive librarian contacted a distance education faculty member to request embedding in his upcoming online Master's course, Topics in Health Care Leadership, and was welcomed. The success of the venture spread and the librarian was asked to embed in additional classes the following semester. Ultimately, "six librarians embedded in numerous classes with multiple sections" (Sullo et al. 2012).

At Miami University Middletown, librarians envisioned an open invitation to participate in the Blackboard embedded librarian pilot for the spring semester of 2009. The e-mailed invitation from three would-be LMS embedded librarians was sent to about 200 full-time and part-time faculty members, on a campus serving 2,700 registered students. Initially, 10 faculty members volunteered to collaborate, teaching 19 sections of 13 different courses across the disciplines, reaching 272 students. The risk of being deluged was real. Yet in the final analysis, the numbers were manageable and none were turned away. Each Miami Middletown librarian collaborated with an average of three faculty members during the pilot.

Planning a Pilot Program

Thinking often leads to doing. Becoming aware of university trends and proposals and how library services can be altered to address these changing conditions is time well spent. Anticipate need. When a university program goes online, it may signal the time has come to pilot an embedded librarian program; consider the University of Central Florida, where "the use of embedded librarians went hand in hand with the development of a Library Research Module for students in online classes" (Bozeman and

Owens 2008, 57). At a public university in Tennessee, "from the embedded service's beginnings: the original distance education librarian closely collaborated with an English instructor to test two online courses" (Hoffman 2011, 448). At the Miami Middletown campus, piloting an embedded librarian program was orchestrated with the launch of the online RN/BSN Bachelor Completion program in 2008–2009.

Creatively meet users' research needs. When librarians sense that current public services are not being fully utilized, it may signal that a new approach is needed. Facing hard truths based on real data may lead to piloting an LMS embedded librarian service. Indeed, in rare instances, faculty initiate the request for an embedded librarian service; this was the case at a public university in Florida. On this campus, "[the] embedded service was developed at [*sic*] regional campus in the university system when one of the instructors requested equal library services for his online course" (Hoffman 2011, 450). Another unmet need at a public university in Arkansas was to ensure more students completed the online English Composition II course successfully; therefore, the service was developed as a way to provide library instruction for the research paper assignment (Hoffmann 2011). Thus, need motivates librarians to pilot embedded librarianship.

Planning an LMS embedded librarian pilot program on your campus begins by taking a first step. In many cases, this necessitates asking questions and gathering ideas and information. Certainly, many decisions must be made as the program is developed.

> In an effort to balance this new offering with an already full array of services, we decided to begin with a pilot involving only volunteer librarians. This allowed us to 'test the waters' to determine if the program would be utilized by course instructors, to calibrate workloads for librarians in the service, and to slowly introduce librarians to the possibility of added responsibilities. (Chesnut, Wesley, and Zai 2010, 125)

Pilots permit tinkering. They are all about risk-taking to enhance delivery of library resources and services for students. They allow for reflection; to note what is working and what can be improved. Give yourself permission to fine-tune the embedded librarianship program as the pilot progresses. Experimentation is standard-operating procedure; few get it right the first time.

Questions to Ask

- What are other librarians at other institutions doing in terms of LMS collaboration with faculty?
- What does LMS embedded librarianship look like at for-profit, non-profit, private, or public institutions?
- Should faculty participation be required by library or university administrators or remain voluntary?
- For that matter, should becoming an LMS embedded librarian be required by the library director or remain voluntary?
- Which librarians ought to participate in the pilot program?
- What library resources and services should become standard offerings?
- How will librarians be matched to faculty willing to collaborate in the information literacy mission?
- Alternatively, should embedded librarians be assigned to departments or programs?

Becoming Informed about Programs and Best Practices

If LMS embedded librarianship is an entirely new service on your college campus, then become informed about the approaches others are taking around the country and world. Learning vicariously spares the novice from expending time, money, and resources. Become informed about best practices in embedded librarianship and thereby avoid mistakes and move ahead with greater confidence.

Several methods of learning about embedded librarianship are available. Professional conferences are a good way to meet those who are engaged in this work. Attendees will see demonstrations of new and emerging technologies. They will be advised by experienced colleagues on the advantages and disadvantages of approaches and software applications and tools by those who may have had to learn through trial and error. They will hear stories of building LMS embedded librarian programs in various geographical areas and at different types of institutions. They will learn how other embedded librarians reach out to distance education users with various results. Much can be gained from the expertise offered and the solutions shared by distance librarians. Networking at conferences may lead to professional relationships that produce rich rewards throughout the year and reach around the globe. For instance, one librarian in Arizona launched a pilot at her own associate-degree-granting institution after attending the 2007 ACRL National Conference where she "repeatedly heard 'embedded librarianship' mentioned. She was interested in trying it out, so she asked an instructor in the Communication/English division to pilot two summer courses" (Hoffman 2011, 451). Ideas can become reality.

Notable conferences to attend:

- The biennial Distance Library Services Conference (formerly known as the Off-Campus Library Services Conference) sponsored by Central Michigan University Libraries is international in scope. It was established in 1982 with the purpose of providing library services to students and faculty away from main campus and online. Papers are published as conference proceedings and also in the *Journal of Library and Information Services in Distance Learning*. See http://ocls.cmich.edu/conf2012.

- The Association of College and Research Libraries Conference of the American Library Association is a biennial event for academic librarians. The Distance Learning Section's purpose is to support off-campus and distance education students. Conference participants may wish to attend its events and join the section. You may also wish to join the Instruction Section, whose mission is to advance information literacy within higher education. ACRL papers are published as conference proceedings and are freely available online. See http://conference.acrl.org.
- The Library Orientation Exchange (LOEX) has existed as an organization for 40 years. It promotes learning, research, and teaching on library instruction and information literacy. Libraries and librarians may become members. It sponsors an annual conference with published proceedings. See www.emich.edu/public/loex/conferences.html.
- State chapters of the Association of College and Research Libraries may also hold annual conferences that address distance learning and embedded librarianship. These chapters may also sponsor a distance learning interest group and specialized workshops. Check with the library organizations within your state or region. For instance, the Academic Library Association of Ohio holds an annual conference. See www.alaoweb.org/conferences/aboutconferences.php. Its Distance Learning Interest Group also offers its own annual workshop: www.alaoweb.org/igs/dlig.

Another means of learning what LMS embedded librarians are doing nationally is to read the professional literature. Consider subscribing to e-mail alerts found in research databases. Create an e-mail alert from a saved search on embedded librarianship in a database such as EBSCOhost's *Library, Information Science, and Technology Abstracts with Full Text* using the following syntax: embedded librarian* AND universities & colleges in (SU Subject Terms). Create a journal alert for new electronic issues of selected journals which publish on the topic:

- *College and Research Libraries News*
- *Information Outlook*

- *Information Today*
- *Journal of Library and Information Services in Distance Learning*
- *LOEX Quarterly*
- *Medical Reference Services Quarterly*
- *Public Services Quarterly*

A third means of gathering information on launching a pilot program is to contact and interview embedded librarians who have a few years of experience. Create a list of questions to ask. Then telephone or e-mail individuals whom you know are working as LMS embedded librarians in your region, whom you have heard present on the topic, or whose articles you have read. Usually librarians are more than willing to share practical information and tips, thereby empowering others to pursue LMS embedded librarianship on their campus.

Building Skills with the LMS

To be effective as an LMS embedded librarian one needs to become aware of the available tools and learn how to use them effectively. This knowledge and experience can be gained in a variety of ways. If you teach a credit course, then you may already possess these building skills. If not, you may be able to take advantage of your institution's professional development opportunities to:

- Attend technology workshops.
- Watch tutorials.
- Consult with an instructional designer on campus.
- Meet with librarians who have these LMS skills.

Then practice using the tools.

- Build a practice course or organization.
- Gather information as needed.
- Use lifelong learning skills to expand your technology expertise.
- Join your university's electronic discussion list to stay current with new developments.

Selecting Services to Offer

During which part of the pilot do instructors want you to interact with students? Anything is possible, but specifying options at the outset may deliver better results. This avoids setting unrealistic expectations that can result in disappointing students and faculty. Begin by asking pilot faculty when they would like an LMS embedded librarian to join the course:

- Only at the start of a term to create content
- During a designated, short-term research period
- Throughout the semester

Factor in what embedded librarians think is workable, given the library staffing situation and librarians' other responsibilities. Estimating how much time embedded librarians can dedicate to the pilot is helpful to all.

What services, research strategies, and library resources do you plan to offer in the LMS? Allow pilot participants to identify high-priority information literacy skills needed to complete the research assignments. Do students need to:

- Understand the research process?
- Develop a topic and research question?
- Find scholarly journal articles, statistics, etc.?
- Learn how to conduct a literature review?
- Cite sources using a specific citation style?

Perhaps the professor has noted particular research deficiencies that reoccur and need to be addressed. You may wish to provide a menu of possible information literacy competencies from which faculty may "order," which will jog the instructors' memories and suggest the scope of what embedded librarians do, as shown in figure 3.1.

Plan to address the information literacy skills that instructors identify as significant. Whether at the initial meeting or prior to the semester's start, request and review research assignments. The objective is to empower students to fulfill course learning outcomes. Recommend relevant sources and strategies. If, in your professional judgment, you foresee potential complications with the research assignment as written, you might suggest possible solutions to the

FIGURE 3.1 Information Literacy Menu

Will Your Students Need To...? [Time Required]	What Will Be Covered	Select Units
Become informed about the Gardner-Harvey Library services & resources [10 minutes]	Library services Library resources Facility	
Develop a search strategy [15 minutes]	Brainstorm a topic Narrow a topic Identify keywords & subject terms Single research question	
Search the online library catalog [15 minutes]	Find book, media, gov docs Access e-books Limiters, sort results, cite item Request item & OhioLINK	
Understand how popular periodicals differ from scholarly journal articles [15 minutes]	Compare & contrast journal vs. magazine articles Peer-review process	
Evaluate websites [20 minutes]	Evaluate websites for credibility Criteria Search engines, portals, & research databases differ	
Cite sources correctly Citation managers [20 minutes]	Explain citation styles: APA, MLA Bibliographic information needed Print, electronic, source type Demo EasyBib, BibMe, FindIt	
Search research databases: Basic [15 minutes]	Academic Search Complete Search techniques Tools: cite, e-mail, abstract, Search terms Find full-text articles: HTML, PDF, FindIt	
Search discipline-specific research databases: Advanced [15 minutes per database]	Subject terms, thesaurus, publication, RSS alerts, field searching & limiters	
Preventing plagiarism [30 minutes]	Citing sources in APA, MLA, etc. Direct quotations Paraphrases Academic integrity	
Research current, controversial issues [30 minutes]	Opposing Viewpoints in Context CQ Researcher Online Primary sources, statistics, local perspective	
Special topics [20–45 minutes]	Statistics, government docs, companies, biographies, digital media, web design	
Literature review [30 minutes]	Research question & process	

Gardner-Harvey Library, Miami University Middletown. Inspired from Radford University, 8/2011.

professor. This strengthens the information-literacy component of the assignment and ensures a better research experience for students.

Your information-literacy expertise enables you to play a starring role in serving students. You know whether new databases have been added to the library collection and which have been dropped, which discovery tools are newly available or no longer in use, and how the library collection is shifting in terms of format or subject areas. Share this information with the instructor and students. Everyone benefits from understanding that the library collection is not static. Economic realities, publishing trends, and emerging technologies all play a role in what embedded librarians are able to bring to the university's teaching and learning mission. Indeed, mixing the assets of an information specialist with a subject specialist is at the heart of embedded librarianship. Students derive greater learning opportunities through this LMS "team-teaching" endeavor. Faculty's burdens are lightened because they can invest more time in teaching, research, and publication within their subject disciplines rather than in information literacy.

Remember that a pilot is a beginning effort. Faculty do not yet understand the full implications of the embedded librarian service. They may hesitate to rely on the embedded librarian and even fear loss of instructional control and esteem in their students' eyes. Time to build trust and win collegial regard is needed. Sometimes instructors do desire a co-instructor relationship that includes having the embedded librarian developing assignments and even grading assignments. At other times, faculty simply desire their online students to benefit from a personalized reference service or accessible library instruction.

Identifying and Recruiting Faculty Collaborators

Once the scope of the embedded librarian pilot is clear, it is time to recruit faculty participants. Soliciting faculty attention and volunteers can be accomplished in various ways. Speak at a faculty meeting, to select departments, or to library enthusiasts with whom you already collaborate. Present at a Center for Teaching and Learning event. Mention the pilot to instructors who regularly visit the library. Invite all full-time and part-time faculty via e-mail.

In an e-mail invitation:

- Use faculty-focused language that signals you understand the pressures of teaching.
- Get quickly to the point that embedded librarians can be part of the solution to students' research efforts and avoid missteps.
- List the advantages of collaborating with an embedded librarian.
- Suggest ways of working together so that faculty can sample embedded librarianship at a level comfortable to them.
- Request essential information: name, course(s), copies of assignments.
- Supply a deadline to stir instructors to action.
- Provide your contact information and indicate when the embedded librarian will communicate again.
- Indicate in general terms the next step faculty and the embedded librarian can expect to take together.
- Be professional, but use appealing humor and word pictures to capture the imagination of what might be possible, as shown in figure 3.2.

Once pilot participants have been identified, embedded librarian assignments can be made. If a librarian acts as departmental liaison, it makes sense to continue that relationship in the pilot. If a librarian already works with certain campus programs, whether honors, graduate, or online, or with particular constituencies such as freshmen or international students, then it makes sense to build on these existing relationships. Matches might also be made on the basis of the embedded librarian's educational degrees, areas of scholarship, or professional experience.

In cases where only one or two librarians will act as embedded librarians, assignments can be made along the lines of the humanities, social sciences, and sciences, or possibly for lower and upper division courses. This reduces workload and limits preparation time. Some librarians, however, may prefer variety and will take on a mix of subjects or lower/upper division courses, or take on different formats: traditional, hybrid, or online. Whatever is decided, the participating librarians make a semester-long commitment to work with assigned instructors.

FIGURE 3.2 Embedded Librarian E-Mail

To: Miami University Middletown Faculty

From: Gardner Harvey Librarians

John Burke, Director; Beth Tumbleson, Assistant Director; Sarah Frye, Public Services Librarian

RE: New Embedded Librarian Program, 2008-2009

If you are a Miami University Middletown faculty member teaching Blackboard, Online, or Off-Campus courses, then this new library service may lighten your academic load. The librarians at the Gardner Harvey Library are offering to collaborate with you as you develop your Blackboard course as it relates to research. Professional librarians trained in information literacy skills and strategies and knowledgeable of the many print and electronic resources made available to Miami University members will create online content and participate in your Blackboard course at a level you designate.

Three Levels of Librarian Participation Are Available:

One: The librarian will create a Library Resources Button and Page in Blackboard.
Librarian will join the Blackboard course as;
Students will be guided to the Library Home Page, relevant electronic resources, online tutorials, websites, and documents on such topics as avoiding plagiarism, citing sources, evaluating websites, etc.

Two: The librarian will join the Blackboard course for a limited time.
Librarian will join the Blackboard course as;
If you plan a research component to your course for a week or more, then the librarian will participate in the course for that period. The librarian will help students navigate the information world and many resources available to Miami University students. Search strategies, search terms, database recommendations, electronic tools and collections might be suggested by the librarian to students after reading student postings or following a Discussion Board thread.

Next, make contact in the new role of embedded librarian by calling or e-mailing faculty members. Offer to meet in person to showcase what is possible and what the content might look like. In this regard, it is sound practice to have an LMS site to demonstrate different tools and content. Seeing options helps faculty envision the possibilities:

- "Ask-the-Librarian" discussion board
- Tutorials on searching databases
- PowerPoint on evaluating websites
- Prezi library orientation of services and resources

If possible, meet in person initially to establish a working relationship. Allow sufficient time for questions and demonstrations and review of library resources that fit course research needs. If in-person meetings are not possible, then meet online, using Elluminate or a similar desktop sharing conference tool. Follow-up conversations can be handled by telephone or in e-mail.

Implementing the Pilot

Typically, a pilot program is run within one term. After the initial collaborative arrangements are made, the work of embedded librarianship begins. The LMS role of embedded librarians varies nationally. Hoffman indicates that while all five academic institutions used the title, "embedded librarian," librarians at four of the five institutions were enrolled under the role of "teaching assistant" (Hoffman 2010, 449). Different learning management systems may use other role status options. What is needed, whatever the system, is enough latitude so that one can add customized library content and interact with enrolled students. For instance, within Blackboard, "instructor" status has access to both the grade book and course analytics which is very helpful when it comes time to assess the pilot. The course builder status, however, permits access to neither, but does allow use of the communication and content creation tools. Give some thought to the status you ideally request within the course, recognizing that faculty may need reassurance and a fuller explanation of needs.

> Faculty response is cautious; many instructors do not like her to take a very active role at first. However, they have becoming (*sic*) increasingly interested in the service, and she is building up her level of trust with them. In fact, she said that since the launch

> of the service, instructors use the library and librarians more. (Hoffman 2011, 451)

Regardless of the role, there are two essential steps to take. First, request the faculty member enroll you in the LMS course. Instructor or course builder roles are ideal. Only then will you have the ability to create content and use the LMS tools. Second, request the instructor send current copies of the research assignments to you. Take time to review them and reflect on possible information literacy solutions and potential sources. What will students need to know and do to complete the assignment? What potential library resources, services, and Web 2.0 tools will aid students in achieving a positive outcome? What research deadlines need to be noted in your calendar to stay ahead of anticipated deadlines? Once this information has been duly processed, the embedded librarian is ready to build content in the LMS.

Include these essential components in the LMS Course:

- Contact information: e-mail, IM, text, telephone, and office location
- Availability: days, hours, or by appointment
- Photo (to personalize the online relationship and a word about yourself)
- Library URL
- Relevant how-to content

Then send a brief announcement or use the LMS mail tool to greet the students and explain your presence and purpose in the course. Later, send timely follow-up search tips you anticipate students might need or other appropriate research strategies. Login to the LMS course at regular intervals to check on course developments. Reply to any e-mail alerts or questions you receive from students. Address any faculty concerns as they unfold. Add new content as needed. If asked by the instructor, provide one-shot instruction or research consultations. In other words, be available and present in the course so that students understand your role as their research guide. In this way, the embedded librarian reaches out to students in their online learning space, where they are more apt to ask research questions or reveal uncertainty about how to execute some aspect of the research assignment.

Survey Tools, Free/ Commercial

QuestionPro–
www.questionpro.com

SurveyGizmo–
www.surveygizmo.com

SurveyMonkey–
www.surveymonkey.com

eSurveysPro–
www.esurveyspro.com

Zoomerang–
www.zoomerang.com

Survey Tools, Commercial

Checkbox–
www.checkbox.com

SurveyGold–
www.surveygold.com

Assessing the Results

Assessment is the final step in implementing the pilot program. Prepare a survey for collaborating faculty and students to determine how the embedded librarian service is being received. Send the survey sometime within the last four weeks of the term prior to final exams so students are more likely to respond with the full experience in mind but before they depart from campus. As a further incentive, work with the instructor to motivate students to complete the survey. Perhaps extra credit can be awarded by the instructor or a pizza party sponsored by the library can be provided to the class section with the highest percentage of completed student returns.

Modifying and Improving

Once survey results have been collected and tallied, as well as personal feedback shared via e-mail or in face-to-face encounters, the embedded librarian pilot may be reviewed honestly and objectively. By listening openly to both negative and positive feedback, the embedded librarian program can be altered and improved. At Northern Kentucky University, embedded librarians in the pilot concluded:

> The success of the first pilot proved that Bb Librarian was definitely a service worth adopting, but it also illuminated ways that Bb Librarian could be further expanded . . . By broadening the program to include online courses without a prerequisite face-to-face session, these distance students are afforded access to the library services that are standard for on-campus students. (Chesnut, Wesley, and Zai 2010, 126)

Other changes eventually followed as well, such as a reduction in desk service by 25 hours weekly and in the Blackboard librarian's service schedule by three hours weekly to allow time for creating resources and interacting with students (Chesnut, Wesley, and Zai 2010). As embedded librarians gain experience working with students in the campus LMS, they have the potential of becoming more effective in delivering timely, customized information literacy instruction.

Given sufficient library staff, faculty willing to collaborate, time, and LMS experience, the embedded librarian service can be sustained and expanded.

Summary

Planning a pilot is critical to the long-term success of LMS embedded librarianship on your campus. If it is carefully conceived, developed, and conducted, the program is more likely to be successful. Establishing a positive partnership between faculty members and librarians is critical. Interacting with students respectfully and professionally builds an appreciative following for the service. Naturally, enhancements and adjustments to the service can be made based upon pilot feedback and changing priorities in the library. Initial success with the pilot will lead to future expansion of the LMS embedded librarian program and the library's alignment with the teaching mission of the university, as well as its commitment to delivering equitable library services to distance faculty and students.

References

Bennett, Erika, and Jennie Simning. 2010. "Embedded Librarians and Reference Traffic: A Quantitative Analysis." *Journal of Library Administration* 50 (5/6): 443–457.

Bozeman, Dee, and Rachel Owens. 2008. "Providing Services to Online Students: Embedded Librarians and Access to Resources." *Mississippi Libraries* 72 (3): 57–59.

Chesnut, Mary Todd, Threasa L. Wesley, and Robert Zai. 2010. "Adding an Extra Helping of Service When You Already Have a Full Plate: Building an Embedded Librarian Program." *Public Services Quarterly* 6 (2/3): 122–129.

Daly, Emily. 2010. "Embedding Library Resources into Learning Management Systems: A Way to Reach Duke Undergrads at Their Points of Need." *College and Research Libraries News* 71 (4): 208–212.

Hoffman, Starr. 2011. "Embedded Academic Librarian Experiences in Online Courses: Roles, Faculty Collaboration and Opinion." *Library Management* 32 (6/7): 444–456.

Sullo, Elaine, Tom Harrod, Gisela Butera, and Alexandra Gomes. 2012. "Rethinking Library Service to Distance Education Students: Analyzing the Embedded Librarian Model." *Medical Reference Services Quarterly* 31 (1): 25–33.

Wright, Laura B., and Ginger H. Williams. 2011. "A History of the Embedded Librarian Program at Odum Library." *Georgia Library Quarterly* 48 (4): 7–11.

Marketing LMS Embedded Librarianship

> Those that do not share knowledge and expertise will find it harder to engage and gain people's attention. Subsequently, they will find themselves bypassed by others that do. (Leboff 2011, 150)

IN THIS CHAPTER:

- ✓ Why Market?
- ✓ LMS Embedded Librarian Survey
- ✓ Marketing: Past and Present
- ✓ Connecting with Faculty
- ✓ Reaching Students
- ✓ Marketing Techniques
- ✓ Summary
- ✓ References

Why Market?

Libraries offer valuable collections, research services, information literacy instruction, and technical support. It is not obvious to users, however, that these offerings are freely and readily available. Many students do not understand how to search proprietary electronic collections and find needed academic information. Faculty may be uncertain how the service benefits their classroom teaching and learning outcomes. Marketing the library's collection, services, and facilities, therefore, has become more important in today's complex information age. LMS embedded librarianship is more likely to be adopted and expanded through marketing.

It is incumbent upon librarians to promote this new mode of information literacy instruction. For the most part, libraries rely on public relations and free publicity rather than paid advertising. In a 21st century, wired world, promoting noteworthy library services is more doable than ever before. Consequently, the authors have chosen to focus on two selected aspects of marketing: public relations and publicity.

LMS Embedded Librarian Survey

In the fall of 2011, Burke and Tumbleson conducted a national LMS embedded librarianship survey, primarily through electronic discussion lists, to which 280 persons responded (see appendix for full details). The results indicated that embedded librarianship is being provided to:

- Traditional, face-to-face LMS courses (182)—69 percent
- Online courses (184)—70 percent
- Hybrid courses (141)—54 percent
- Undergraduate LMS courses (160)—61 percent
- Graduate LMS courses (110)—42 percent

The LMS embedded librarian service is a recent development at many institutions, according to survey results. Respondents began the program:

- One year ago or less (41)—15 percent
- One to two years ago (50)—18 percent
- Two to three years ago (49)—18 percent
- Four or more years ago (50)—18 percent

These are positive signs! Librarians continue to explore and offer reference service and information literacy instruction through LMS embedded librarianship.

Among survey respondents, certain promotional methods were favored. Note the numbers below:

- Word-of-mouth marketing (WOMM) (180)—70 percent
- Personal invitation by librarians (174)—67 percent
- E-mail by librarians (168)—65 percent
- Library brochures (73)—28 percent
- Library blogs (37)—14 percent

With limited resources and staff time, where should marketing efforts be directed to garner the greatest return on investment?

Key Terms

Marketing: Promoting and selling an organization's products and services to customers

Public relations: Efforts to generate free media coverage and influence the public to view an organization favorably

Publicity: News item or story by mass media outlets to attract the public's attention

Advertising: Paid mass media communication by a sponsor to promote, persuade, and sell its products and services

Marketing: Past and Present

> Obviously, the choices for finding information have multiplied and exploded in the past fifteen years, and libraries no longer have a monopoly on information. In other words, we are no longer the gatekeepers of information. In marketing terms, we need to reposition our brand. We need to find ways to raise awareness of our vital role in our communities and articulate the role that libraries play in the new information landscape. (Dowd, Evangeliste, and Silberman 2010, 130)

Marketing methods have changed over time. Marketing authority Philip Kotler traces this passage from Marketing 1.0 in the industrial age, which was product-centric, to today's Marketing 2.0 in the information age, which is consumer-oriented, to Marketing 3.0 in the values-driven era, which touches the human spirit (Kotler, Kartajaya, and Setiawan 2010, 6). Traditionally, the marketing mix has concentrated on the "four Ps:" products and services, place, price, and promotion. Walters notes that libraries should also consider two more P's: positioning and politics, and goes on to discuss the "Six Ps" strategies (Walters 2004, 71). Often, Walters includes a success story to illustrate each strategy.

In *Marketing Today's Academic Library,* Mathews also notes how library marketing methods have changed. Promotional campaigns today should "be engaging. This is a shift away from the more traditional transaction-based approach and instead highlights the experiential narrative" (Mathews 2009, 2). Mathews maintains that library advertising should focus on the lifestyle of students. According to Mathews, academic library marketing campaigns today need to be: "tangible, experiential, relatable, measureable, shareable, and surprising" (Mathews 2009, 4).

The Six Ps

- Products and Services
- Place
- Price
- Promotion
- Positioning and Repositioning
- Public Policy and Politics

(Walters 2004, 71)

Leboff, another marketing author, also distinguishes between the old marketing approach and the current one. He concurs with Mathews that transactions no longer signify, and that "[the] battle in the marketplace is no longer for transactions. Rather, it is for attention. Quite simply, those companies with customer attention win" (Leboff 2011, 40). Formerly, commercial marketing campaigns relied on "billboards, magazines, newspapers, radio, television, direct mail, cold calls" (Leboff 2011, 131). Businesses protected and controlled information. Those in marketing did not hesitate to intrude and invade; they would shout, interrupt, and propagandize. In contrast, Leboff recommends alternative marketing strategies today which emphasize conversation, authenticity, and values, noting that establishing "credibility and demonstrating expertise and knowledge, by supplying good content, will enhance your reputation" (Leboff 2011, 134). LMS embedded librarians should continue to ask what value they are providing.

Providing value in terms of information research concepts and strategies that students need is why embedded librarians show up in the LMS. Sharing strategies, tools, and library resources is the goal. In this way, an embedded librarian earns a reputation as a trusted research consultant. Students value the personal guide who communicates clearly and enables them to negotiate the Internet and their institution's library system. Google only goes so far. Students want answers to their personal research dilemmas and questions. They want authenticity in their relationships, a hallmark of the Internet age. They believe that the "move towards genuine, authentic and real is another result of the internet-enabled world in which we now live, and the move from image to reputation" (Leboff 2011, 134). Being a credentialed information specialist with years of experience is no longer enough to win over an admiring following. The embedded librarian must be seen as open and honest in his interactions with students.

Becoming attractive to end-users is the essential message in advertising LMS embedded librarianship. That attractiveness relies upon two elements: being noticed and imparting value (Leboff 2011, 99). Once the academic community notices the LMS embedded librarianship service and realizes its value to their own goals, the program is in a position to prosper. Knowing what users need and appreciate will grow the embedded librarian service.

Connecting with Faculty

In order to publicize the embedded librarian service to faculty, you need to walk a mile in their shoes, as the saying goes. Adopt the instructor's mindset. Instructors are versed in the research and practice associated with their subject disciplines. They are less comfortable presenting the changing research tools and resources that the university library offers. When database interfaces are updated or vendors buy and merge databases, librarians are more likely to be notified before faculty. Professors understand the library's potential usefulness to students, but on their own many are not prepared to do more than link to the library website or send students to the library. Therein lies the value of the LMS embedded librarian who shows up and offers to collaborate as needed with the instructor. How many professors will turn down a helping hand once they judge that the librarian is knowledgeable, possesses technology skills, and, most importantly, interacts kindly with their students? Attracting attention, becoming known, and being valued is your challenge. Engage professors as customers, because a "customer engagement model focuses on giving value around the product or services you deliver . . . In this way, you become 'sticky' or attractive" (Leboff 2011, 46).

Marketing is ongoing. Instructors come and go, curricular needs and priorities change, and course formats (classroom, hybrid, or online) are altered. At the close of each academic year, April through June, e-mail faculty and invite them to participate in the upcoming academic year. Then you will have time during the slower summer season to create additional customized content. Another call for participation might be sent a month before the fall term begins, to reach newly hired faculty or simply to serve as a reminder for those who have not yet responded. At this time, professors may be returning to campus and working on their courses. They may be ready for a fresh approach and be open to enlisting the services of an LMS embedded librarian. Figure 4.1 shows a sample call to participate in a program.

Send faculty reminders through the first week of the term in case they would like to join the program. Be open to accepting faculty members who express interest mid-term, as they consider how best to support their students during the research project period. Share the message in these ways:

- Presentation at a faculty meeting or an academic council meeting
- Library or institutional newsletter promotional article
- Description of the service on the library website

Each year, from November through January, market the service while instructors are still on campus finishing coursework and giving final exams. More instructors may be interested in a spring semester LMS embedded librarian, as they prepare to teach new courses or

FIGURE 4.1 Embedded Librarians Want You!

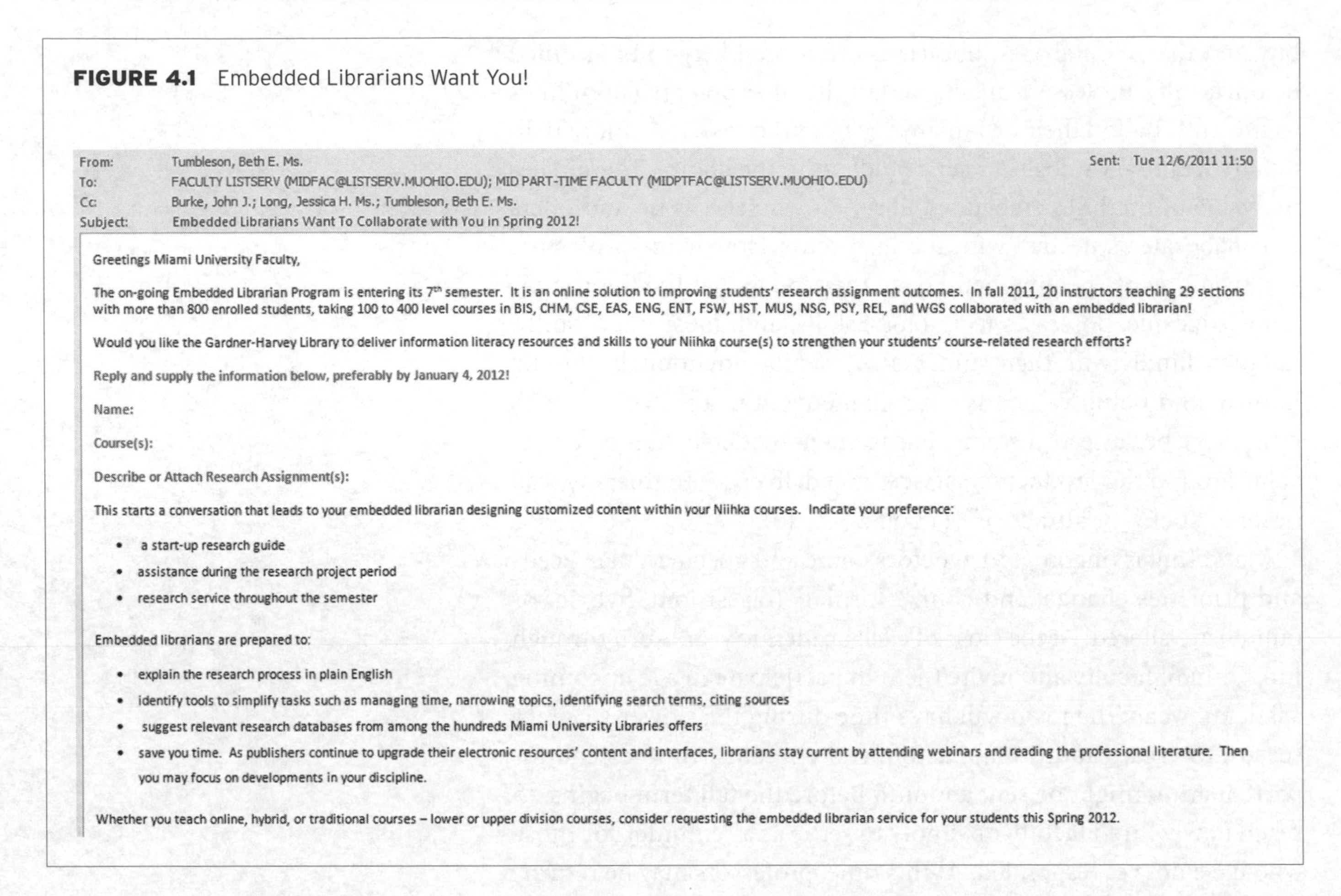

From: Tumbleson, Beth E. Ms. Sent: Tue 12/6/2011 11:50
To: FACULTY LISTSERV (MIDFAC@LISTSERV.MUOHIO.EDU); MID PART-TIME FACULTY (MIDPTFAC@LISTSERV.MUOHIO.EDU)
Cc: Burke, John J.; Long, Jessica H. Ms.; Tumbleson, Beth E. Ms.
Subject: Embedded Librarians Want To Collaborate with You in Spring 2012!

Greetings Miami University Faculty,

The on-going Embedded Librarian Program is entering its 7th semester. It is an online solution to improving students' research assignment outcomes. In fall 2011, 20 instructors teaching 29 sections with more than 800 enrolled students, taking 100 to 400 level courses in BIS, CHM, CSE, EAS, ENG, ENT, FSW, HST, MUS, NSG, PSY, REL, and WGS collaborated with an embedded librarian!

Would you like the Gardner-Harvey Library to deliver information literacy resources and skills to your Niihka course(s) to strengthen your students' course-related research efforts?

Reply and supply the information below, preferably by January 4, 2012!

Name:

Course(s):

Describe or Attach Research Assignment(s):

This starts a conversation that leads to your embedded librarian designing customized content within your Niihka courses. Indicate your preference:

- a start-up research guide
- assistance during the research project period
- research service throughout the semester

Embedded librarians are prepared to:

- explain the research process in plain English
- identify tools to simplify tasks such as managing time, narrowing topics, identifying search terms, citing sources
- suggest relevant research databases from among the hundreds Miami University Libraries offers
- save you time. As publishers continue to upgrade their electronic resources' content and interfaces, librarians stay current by attending webinars and reading the professional literature. Then you may focus on developments in your discipline.

Whether you teach online, hybrid, or traditional courses – lower or upper division courses, consider requesting the embedded librarian service for your students this Spring 2012.

redesign research assignments. Perhaps they have heard how helpful the service is from colleagues.

Reaching Students

Connect with students. In a word, advertise: sell library stuff.

> Although we refer to it by different names including outreach, communication, advocacy or public relations, academic libraries are unquestionably trying to reach their students. But is it working? My research reveals that most of these efforts are inconsistent, fragmented, and largely go without assessment (Mathews 2009, 6)

Many of the listed shortcomings are avoided by LMS embedded librarians. Students are already logged on their professors' LMS courses and reading their assignments. By placing customized research help next to the assignment or on a separate embedded librarian page, students have access to streamlined, credible sources and research strategies. The embedded librarian also has access to announcements, the discussion board, forum, blog, wiki, and the mail tool, and can dialogue with students about their research questions. They also have access to course analytics to determine when and how many students are using the embedded librarian content. Being able to communicate quickly with the entire class or just with one student online is powerful.

A word of caution is in order. Be careful not to overload students with too much information. Let students know how they can further develop research skills with the embedded librarian's assistance by:

- Attending a synchronous chat session
- Watching a digital tutorial
- Posting a question in a discussion board
- Using an instant messaging widget

Nor do you want to make contact too frequently and be perceived as an annoyance and an intruder. Eventually, you will develop a working relationship, and students may even begin to seek you out personally whenever they have a research question and you "become one of their trusted sources of information" (Leboff 2011, 45). Once students discover your value as a personal research coach, you become real to them and "sticky." They will spread the word among their friends.

Once in the LMS, promote the service to students. Introduce yourself and explain what you are able to offer. Introduce yourself briefly, provide contact information, explain your presence and purpose in the course, and your value to students. Become informed about the academic calendar and social events that affect campus life. Mathews advises librarians to consider users' schedules and habits, and include "orientations, popular sporting events, mid-terms, finals, and deadlines for major assignments. A calendar view allows you to monitor the student mindset" (Mathews 2009, 144). Do enter key research assignment deadlines from the course syllabus on your calendar, and send out student search tips or tools one to two weeks ahead of each deadline for the courses in which you are embedded. Students often tune in on a need-to-know basis. It is also gratifying to receive a specific research question, sent as a reply, on a saved class e-mail sent weeks before. Students will communicate when they are ready. As Leboff reminds his readers, "The point is that customers and prospects want to interact on their terms . . . Wherever they are is where you should be" (Leboff 2011, 43). Students work online, in their familiar LMS course sites; when they are ready to research and write prior to due date, they surface. Be prepared to interact.

Address the "so what" factor. Tell faculty and students explicitly how the program will add value or benefit them. When stakeholders recognize you are willing to give them time and knowledgeable assistance with their course-related research and that the exchange is conducted with warmth, empathy, and respect, they are likely to respond very favorably.

10 Selling Points of LMS Embedded Librarianship

1. Personal librarian within complex library system
2. Embedded librarian familiar with the research assignment
3. Online research expertise within the familiar LMS
4. Easy mechanism for asking questions
5. Highly relevant library content
6. Quick links to electronic resources, not the whole library website
7. Clear explanations of library jargon
8. Search strategies and tips
9. How-to digital tutorials
10. Web 2.0 tools for mind mapping, presenting, citing sources

Marketing Techniques

As noted earlier, promoting library services can be accomplished using a variety of marketing strategies. Some rely on stakeholders, like word-of-mouth marketing; others on library staff. Some approaches are free or low-cost. Intentionally promoting LMS embedded librarians does not have to cost what advertising firms typically charge, especially if Web 2.0 social networking tools are employed. What is required is a willingness to publicize the service using meaningful methods.

Word-of-Mouth Marketing

Word-of-mouth marketing (WOMM) works! It is affordable yet powerful; it "centers on the concept that 10 percent of the population influences the behavior of the other 90 percent" (Dowd, Evangeliste, and Silberman 2010, 3). Once people become passionate about a service, they tell others.

LMS embedded librarianship lends itself to WOMM when anxious students finally encounter someone who understands academic research, the library's collections, the specifics of their research assignment, and is available to consult online. This is especially true when their professor endorses and refers them to the embedded librarian. In this way the embedded librarian becomes a part of the class. Because people will "trust the recommendations from people they know over those of a stranger" WOMM creates relationships by employing "a virtual connection, sometimes between people who have never met each other face-to-face (Dowd, Evangeliste, and Silberman 2010, 3–4).

WOMM

The reasoning behind WOMM began as a simple concept. Produce a product that people can be passionate about, get it into the hands of those people whose opinion other people respect, give the influencers the tools to share their satisfaction, and let them influence people they know and drive people to use your product.

(Dowd, Evangeliste, and Silberman 2010, 5)

How true of LMS embedded librarianship! Not only will students refer friends to the embedded librarian, but faculty may promote the program with equal fervor to colleagues. Person-to-person recommendations strengthen the program more than any article the library will ever post.

Creating a Story That Attracts Collaboration

Contemporary publicity and advertising campaigns are incorporating storytelling (see Daniel Pink's chapter on "Story" in *A Whole New Mind* [2005]). Storytelling is powerful; it is an ancient and proven way to gain partners: "A compelling story can be engaging in itself. It allows people to understand you. In turn, this makes it easier for them to feel that they know you and can trust you" (Leboff 2011, 98). Once that bond of trust is established, end-users will contact and collaborate with you. They will even spread the message that LMS embedded librarians add value to the course. In this way, librarians' reputations are enhanced and become recognized players in the academic mission. Stories are memorable while statistics are soon forgotten. University administrators may be impressed by numbers and percentages, but the larger academic community only yawns. Library advocacy can best be advanced through sharing stories.

Quick Tips

- Interesting
- Touching, Emotional Experience
- Conflict and Resolution
- Genuine, Real
- Short, Simple
- Understands Users' Needs
- Supports the Library
- Beginning, Middle, End

What elements make a strong story for publicity? Dowd, Evangeliste, and Silberman (2010) share some pointers:

Clearly, a library benefits from

> story-driven marketing strategies . . . As a result libraries should embark upon their marketing efforts by first developing and drafting a service story. The service story, drafted as an internal strategic marketing document for use by all staff, serves as a road-map for virtually every imaginable patron interaction as well as efforts aimed at marketing or promoting library services. It allows library staff to effectively sell, up-sell and cross-sell the relevant library services to specific sets of customers at the most appropriate time. (Germano 2010, 7)

Testimonials differ from stories in that they are written remarks by satisfied customers who applaud the staff or service. Stories are more personal; they "take testimonies to the next level and show that positive experience had an impact on a person's life" (Dowd, Evangeliste, and Silberman 2010, 27). Keep updating your stories as conditions change and improve at your institution. Use stories to support and promote the LMS embedded librarian service, wherever they are publicized: library website, blog, or brochure.

No-Cost Marketing

These days library budgets are under scrutiny. There is little money earmarked for marketing; "budgets rarely, if ever, have a specific line item for marketing or promotional campaigns. Library school curricula at virtually all ALA-accredited programs have no required marketing course" (Germano 2010, 6). Making a personal presentation can be an effective marketing strategy. Consider presenting and explaining the LMS embedded librarian service to faculty at orientations, department meetings, Center for Teaching and Learning sessions, or appropriate conferences via poster sessions, tech spots, or delivering papers. Speaking professionally about this new information literacy method may capture their interest and elicit buy-in. Give voice to the value of LMS embedded librarianship.

Blogging

- Benefits: Free, Instant, and Easy, Visual Appeal via Photos and Videos, Analytics
- Quick Tips: Guiding Theme, Short, Personal Voice, Good Grammar, Controversy is OK, Guest Writers, Share and Comment Tools

(Dowd, Evangeliste, and Silberman 2010, 85-87)

Employ online and Web 2.0 social networking tools. These online tools are accessible and free. Post a newsworthy item, success story, digital video, or image to Blogger, Twitter, Flickr, Facebook, a LinkedIn group, or YouTube. Utilize your institution's communication channels. Use your campus e-mail to invite potential professors to partner in the program. Place a banner ad on the library website. Promote the service in the library blog or university wiki through a service story that stirs the imagination.

Reuse these links and Web 2.0 products on the library website. Send them to potential faculty, information technology personnel, or university e-learning administrators who may welcome more information about providing equitable access to library resources and services.

Low-Cost Marketing

There are low-cost techniques to promote the program. In a review of Mathews' work, Cullen summarizes the options:

> Matthews [*sic*] lists common communication strategies used by academic libraries: print materials (fliers, bookmarks,

> posters, floor plans, newsletters), giveaways (pens, magnets, USB drives), events (orientations, workshops, contests, film viewings), campus media, digital media (library website, blogs, podcasts, social networking sites) and world of mouth. (Cullen 2010, 69)

Make certain to highlight embedded librarians as a valued library service through any of the aforementioned library artifacts which can be given away.

Library and college publications are another viable means of converting campus constituencies without expending large sums beyond staff time and printing. Publish library brochures, newsletters, bookmarks, or posters for LMS embedded librarianship. Distribute them in the library. Use campus bulletin boards too. Personally visit faculty in their offices during finals with a message stuffed in a fortune cookie, as was done at the University of Wisconsin, Eau Claire's McIntyre Library (Jennings and Tvaruzka 2010), or taped to candy during "crunch" time.

Summary

Marketing LMS embedded librarianship will contribute to an expanding program. Employ a variety of publicity strategies. Through repeated explanations of its benefits, word-of-mouth marketing among faculty and students, shared success stories, personal invitations to participate, and Web 2.0 posts, campus constituencies will come to hear of the service. More instructors and students will be open to interacting with the embedded librarian in the LMS. In time, they will come to understand the value an embedded librarian is able to offer in connection with course-related research assignments. This seeming stranger is aware of recent library collection additions, possesses in-depth knowledge of database features, offers tested search strategies, guides users around technology pitfalls, and is approachable online. Who would have guessed that such a library service was available and worked well, until it was touted on campus and personally tested? Creative publicity about this new information-literacy method ensures the continued growth of the LMS embedded librarian program on your campus.

References

Cullen, Michael. 2010. "Marketing Today's Academic Library: A Bold New Approach to Communicating with Students." *Australian Library Journal* 59 (1/2): 68–70.

Dowd, Nancy, Mary Evangeliste, and Jonathan Silberman. 2010. *Bite-Sized Marketing: Realistic Solutions for the Overworked Librarian.* Chicago: American Library Association.

Germano, Michael A. 2010. "Narrative-Based Library Marketing: Selling your Library's Value during Tough Economic Times." *Bottom Line: Managing Library Finances* 23 (1): 5–17.

Jennings, Eric, and Kathryn Tvaruzka. 2010. "Quick and Dirty Library Promotions That Really Work." *Journal of Library Innovation* 1 (2): 6–14.

Kotler, Philip, and Nancy Lee. 2007. *Marketing in the Public Sector: A Roadmap for Improved Performance.* Upper Saddle River, NJ: Wharton School Publishing.

Kotler, Philip, Hermawan Kartajaya, and Iwan Setiawan. 2010. *Marketing 3.0: From Products to Customers to the Human Spirit.* Hoboken, NJ: Wiley.

Leboff, Grant. 2011. *Sticky Marketing: Why Everything in Marketing Has Changed and What to Do about It.* London, UK: Kogan Page.

Mathews, Brian. 2009. *Marketing Today's Academic Library: A Bold New Approach to Communicating with Students.* Chicago: American Library Association.

Pink, Daniel H. 2005. *A Whole New Mind: Moving from the Information Age to the Conceptual Age.* New York: Riverhead Books.

Walters, Suzanne. 2004. *Library Marketing that Works.* New York: Neal-Schuman Publishers.

Building the Embedded Librarian Presence

Instructional Content and Instructional Design

IN THIS CHAPTER:

Starting with a Plan

Embedded librarianship may be attempted on a trial basis, perhaps with just a few pilot courses for a semester. It lends itself to experimentation, applying aspects and services learned from conference presentations and case studies in the literature. Experiments should always be a part of library work, whether in the LMS or not, but in order to take the service beyond the pilot stage and to keep it evolving to meet the developing expectations of students and faculty there needs to be a formalized structure to guide its design. Embedded librarians need a planning process to successfully build instructional content and implement it in the LMS.

Putting that plan to work will lead the embedded librarian into decisions about what content to include in the LMS. Some content will be readily at hand, perhaps in the form of handouts or step-by-step instructions that can be added into the LMS or databases that can be linked. Other content will need to be created, such as video tutorials demonstrating databases or how to narrow a research topic. Finally, there may be content available from other libraries that can be reused in your setting.

One way to look at this situation of design and creation is to consider what embedded librarianship might look like at your institution. Back in chapter 1, a list of characteristics and services found in embedded librarianship was shared, drawn from the authors' survey of embedded librarians (see appendix for a summary of results). That list is reproduced below:

- Encouragement to contact the embedded librarian for further reference assistance
- Links to library databases and other information resources within the course
- Individual librarian is assigned to one or more participating courses
- Library tab or link to the library website appears in the LMS for all courses
- Tutorials, either embedded or linked, in the course
- Information on research concepts (i.e., scholarly vs. popular periodicals, plagiarism, citing sources)
- Suggested research strategies for course assignments
- Instant messaging or chat widgets in the course
- Interactive sessions with classes using web conferencing software (Adobe Connect, Elluminate, Wimba, WebEx, etc.)
- Synchronous chats with groups of students

This is not an exhaustive list of all that can be done in the embedded classroom or course site, but it reflects the most common elements included in embedded librarian programs. You can use a list like this to pick out the pieces that might work well in your setting. You can also use it to help you brainstorm and get into the mindset of what bringing library instruction into the LMS might look like. Coming up with an image of what the service could mean to your students and faculty and how it might fit into the other offerings of your library can be very motivating and inspire your development.

This list is even more valuable, though, if it causes you to ask a key question: how were these methods chosen and then implemented in various embedded librarian environments? Part of the story is the experimentation and sampling phenomenon noted above. Beyond that, in many cases the embedded librarians involved also made careful choices among the available services and options to best meet the needs of groups of students and individual courses. That leads to the next question: how can you structure your own pursuit of the best embedded librarian services that meet your local needs?

The ADDIE Model

One way to organize these choices into a flow is to use the ADDIE model. ADDIE is a model of instructional system design that seeks to arrange the learning environment to meet learning outcomes and measure them. It is used widely in instructional design work and provides the foundation for several other models. The acronym ADDIE stands for Analysis, Design, Development, Implementation, and Evaluation. It is helpful to take a look at the process of designing materials for a course with an embedded librarian through the lens of these phases of design. Even if librarians lack the time to formally follow an instructional design process, understanding ADDIE can get them thinking about the best ways to achieve the outcomes they are pursuing (Bell and Shank 2007). The pages that follow will incorporate questions, issues, steps, and decision-points that fit into the five parts of ADDIE.

The ADDIE Model of Instructional System Design

- Analysis
- Design
- Development
- Implementation
- Evaluation

Analysis

The Analysis phase helps the embedded librarian determine the requirements for a given course. It is effectively gathering background information about the course, the assignments, and the students that can help inform the design decisions the embedded librarian needs to make. Strickland (2012) offers many useful questions to ask in the Analysis stage when designing whole courses, several of which have relevance to embedded librarianship. Focusing directly on embedded librarianship, there are several possible questions to ask at this point in the process, including:

- What does the instructor expect students to do in the course vis-à-vis research or information literacy activities?
- What do students in the course already know about using the library or locating information related to their assignments (i.e., is this the second course in a sequence where the first course already identified general research tools in the discipline)?
- Which resources make sense to introduce in the course? Which ones are essential?
- How is the course being taught? What options will the librarian have for interacting with students?
- When is the research assignment due? What timeline are the students operating under as they build toward completing the assignment?

- Are there points in the flow of the class where it would be useful to share research tips or teach information literacy skills to help students prepare for the work ahead?

The main idea of this phase is to get as clear a picture of the class as possible. As noted earlier in the book, the picture available to the embedded librarian is bound to be more complete than the typical view afforded to an instruction librarian. The typical instruction request from a faculty member comes with a focus on a single upcoming assignment, or perhaps on the need to cover multiple assignments in the discipline, but all within a single class session with the librarian. The librarian will normally be provided with an assignment document and possibly a copy of the syllabus. By approaching library instruction for the class as a more collaborative process with the faculty member, and having access to more course documents and communications between faculty and students, the embedded librarian is able to approach the course with more than a single assignment/single class meeting connection. Three specific ways to approach analysis are:

- Discuss the course with the faculty member.
- Analyze the instructional needs of a course.
- Analyze student needs.

Discuss the Course with the Faculty Member

A crucial first step to analysis with embedded classes is to have a discussion with the faculty member to determine what research skills and knowledge are needed for students to succeed in the course. Faculty members will know the range of assignments in the course, and will also be able to share trouble spots that students have experienced in the past. As librarians receive requests to embed, the next step is to gather information from the faculty member, whether through a face-to-face conversation, an exchange of e-mail, or through a survey. Multiple methods may be used, such as having faculty fill out an initial survey (as profiled in chapter 3) and then having a follow-up conversation to work out the best strategy for implementing embedded librarian services.

Analyze the Instructional Needs of a Course

What is the instructor hoping for students to learn in the course, and to what degree are any of these objectives related to information literacy skills? Once there is a conversation with the faculty member and the librarian has the chance to study course documents, there will be a clearer sense of what the coursework entails and how information literacy enters into the situation. The librarian can also call on her expertise with similar course interactions to consider options for instructional tools and resources that will ease students' paths. This is a great point to bring together the facts the librarian knows about the course and start brainstorming about possible resources and approaches to reach and instruct students.

Analyze Student Needs

Student needs are strongly related to the area of analyzing the instructional requirements of the course, but one must also take into account issues related to the course level and expectations for students' preparation. If the course is the second or third part of a sequence of courses, students may already have a fundamental understanding of library resources and approaches to similar assignments. On the other hand, an introductory course may draw students who are new to academic research and will likely need a broader array of explanations and suggestions of resources. In addition, there are always courses that involve students from a mix of backgrounds who may have experience with earlier coursework but as a group may have a more scattered understanding of library research. It can be extremely helpful to learn from the faculty member about barriers or difficulties that students have faced in the past. While every group of students is different, these difficulties with tasks or with learning skills can be areas for the librarian to concentrate on.

He's Making a List, and Checking It Twice

One way to summarize this analysis would be to create, either on paper, in virtual form, or just mentally, a list of the goals that the embedded librarian has for the course. What has to happen in this semester for the embedded librarian to feel successful? At this point, prior to the actual implementation of materials and interactions, it is not possible to guarantee results or predict what students will or will not achieve in their research projects. But it is useful to sketch out even a short list of the intended outcomes for the information literacy elements of the course that can help in the Design and Development phases of the ADDIE process. This list can also be useful in the final Evaluation phase as well.

For example, say that the embedded librarian is working with an introductory psychology class for the upcoming semester. It is a traditional face-to-face course in which the instructor uses the LMS to house course documents, post and collect some assignments, and hold online asynchronous discussions with students. From a conversation with the faculty member, the librarian learns that students will be expected to complete an article search assignment early in the semester, and then write a five to seven page paper on a psychology topic in the latter part of the course. Further study of the assignment documents and the syllabus shows that students will be guided toward a specific topic, using a directed periodical database, for the first assignment, and will need to properly create an APA citation for the article. The lengthier assignment will involve students using discipline-related databases to find scholarly sources (primarily articles) on a topic of the student's choosing. So, to summarize the expectations for this course, one can create the following list of abilities that students will need to have to succeed with the assignments:

- How to find, navigate, and use the PsycINFO database
- How to create citations in APA format
- Be able to identify scholarly sources and differentiate them from popular sources
- Know other psychology periodical databases to search
- Be able to create a bibliography and use in-text citations in APA format

This list will set the course for the next phase of instructional design.

Design

The next phase of ADDIE is Design. Design is where the embedded librarian's plan comes together. In this phase, the librarian brings together the data gathered in the Analysis phase, adds in personal knowledge of library resources and research skills that will be helpful for students, and researches additional resources or methods to use in the embedded classroom. The end result is a plan for building an embedded librarian presence in the course site.

Approaching the Embedded Component as a Course within a Course

One way to think about the embedded presence in the Design phase is to imagine the library instruction and resource segment of the course as a unified set of material within the course. That is, the set of embedded library instructional materials, the links to library services and library databases, and the personal assistance of the librarian must all work together to teach students in the course the skills and resources that have been identified in the Analysis phase. The embedded librarian collaborates with the faculty member to add information literacy components to the broader content of the course. In this process, though, it is easy to lose the librarian-supplied materials among the larger picture of the course. However these segments are allocated within the online classroom or course site, be sure to examine them so that they have a coherency that helps students learn key information literacy concepts along with their course materials. As much as librarians should engage in the larger course, they need to ensure that their contributions are relevant and helpful.

What does this examination look like? In some embedded librarian presences within a course, the materials may be located in a single area (e.g., on a single page or tab within the course). It would be easy to look at the resources and contact information chosen for inclusion in this page or area and tick them off as the librarian reviews the instructional goals she intends to meet within the course. Similarly, it may be valuable to create a list of the resources and approaches the embedded librarian intends to use in the course that semester, and then compare them to the intended set of goals. This is useful to include content that may not be listed in a single spot in the LMS, such as content that is listed next to an instructor's description of an assignment, or the use of a discussion board or other LMS tools by the embedded librarian. In either event, there should be some review of the content that the embedded librarian is going to place in the course and the other means that the librarian will use to communicate with students.

Using the example of the psychology class and the list of goals in the previous phase of instructional design, imagine that the embedded librarian has come up with the following list of content, resources, and activities to include in the course:

- Multiple means of contact information for the librarian and/or other library staff
- A link to the PsycINFO database
- A link to APA citation guidance and/or an example of an article citation and/or a tutorial on APA citations
- Information on how to distinguish scholarly sources from popular sources
- Links to other psychology databases
- Information and guidance on bibliographies and in-text citations in APA, either through a link, content written within the course, a tutorial, or some combination of these
- Creation of a forum or a discussion board topic within the LMS classroom for the librarian to take questions from students
- A face-to-face library instruction session with students

You could then use the list developed at the end of the Analysis phase above to assess the activities above. That list of goals is reproduced below, with a note on whether each goal was covered by the plan:

- How to find, navigate, and use the PsycINFO database—covered by the link in the LMS, content located in the LMS (possibly including a tutorial), and perhaps a face-to-face library instruction session
- How to create citations in APA format—covered by content located in the LMS or links to tutorials or other resources
- Be able to identify scholarly sources and differentiate them from popular sources—covered by content located in the LMS or links to tutorials or other resources
- Know other psychology periodical databases to search—covered by links in the LMS, content located in the LMS, and perhaps the face-to-face library instruction session
- Be able to create a bibliography and use in-text citations in APA format—covered by content located in the LMS or links to tutorials or other resources

Deciding Which Resources to Focus on and Which Skills to Teach and Reinforce

A further word on selecting resources and instructional materials may be helpful. Instructional librarians are always faced with the temptation of sharing more resources than will comfortably fit in the confines of a 50 or 75 minute instruction session. The same goes for the myriad of tips and suggestions that a given class could benefit from. The confines of time force the wise librarian to concentrate on the key resources to show and share, perhaps listing additional resources on a handout for later review. The embedded librarian presence is not under the same limitations of time, and the LMS presents seemingly endless amounts of space to include links to databases, the catalog, websites, tutorials, and other resources, along with a narrative that explains concepts and gives navigational guidance to get around the suggested resources. This arrangement does provide an excellent opportunity for the embedded librarian to be able to share a few more resources given the increased time available in the embedded course. But it can also lead the librarian to consider going not just the extra mile, but the extra marathon.

Do not give in to this temptation! When the embedded librarian is in the Design phase, it is a great time to think seriously about the key resources that will be needed. It may also be the time to consider some secondary resources that might be helpful and would need to be left out of a one-time instruction session or a handout. Much of that consideration will depend upon the expectations of the class and the breadth of research choices available to students in the course. As the embedded librarian brainstorms items to include in the course site, it is helpful to sketch out the possibilities and then review them to decide which are absolutely necessary and which are optional. It may become clear from that list that the entire group of possibilities is just too deep to be accessible to students, and truly useful resources may get lost in the mess of options. One way to include a larger number of resources is to stagger the inclusion or revelation of groups of resources to match the needs of the current assignment (by actively editing documents or resource lists, or through the automated appearance or disappearance of course documents that can be set through the LMS). There may be times in the upcoming Development phase to return to this list and expand the final list of resources and instructional materials, but it is better to start out with the basics until it is known how the embedded librarian presence will function.

Development

Development is the phase where the embedded librarian makes the final plan for laying out links and content in the LMS and builds and locates instructional materials. All the information-gathering, brainstorming, and planning leads to this stage, when the librarian readies and creates materials that will serve the embedded class. Final decisions on the items to include as part of the embedded presence will be made now, though there is still time for tweaking them in the Implementation phase. In addition to creating the final list, there are three important elements of this phase: (1) building content, (2) finding existing content, and (3) writing narrative content. Each one is addressed below in turn, and together will help prepare a librarian for the Implementation phase.

Building Your Own Content and Learning Objects

The content that an embedded librarian includes in the LMS needs to reflect the local collection of resources and services that the library provides. This is not to say that content or learning objects created elsewhere cannot be used, and this approach to adding embedded content will be addressed in a moment. But there is much to be said for creating materials that are focused on the course, that incorporate instructional materials and links to resources that best fit the needs of the students, and that allow for a personal connection to the embedded librarian. The following types of content are ones for the librarian to consider building as she develops the elements chosen in the Design phase.

The Embedded Librarian Landing Page

No matter how you approach organizing content in an embedded course, it makes sense to have a spot where students can readily turn to quickly click on links to databases, access tutorials or other instructional content, and find contact information to ask questions of their embedded librarian. The page is generally linked among the other tools or content locations in the course site, usually on the menu of options found on the left side of the screen. It may be titled "Embedded Librarian" or "Ask Your Librarian" or whatever makes sense for the given institution. How much information the librarian locates at this spot may vary. An alternative to putting all library-related content in this spot is to locate other information among the assignments or subject-related content pages in the course site. That option is addressed in the following section, but however one divides up the embedded content there should be a central place that advertises library services.

A common arrangement of the embedded librarian page is shown below in figure 5.1. A welcome message from the embedded librarian is followed by various forms of contact information. This is followed by the arrangement of useful resources and instructional materials needed for the course. A variety of approaches can be used here, from listing out all of the essential resources right on the page, to creating subcategories (e.g., "Finding Articles," or "Learning How to Cite Sources in Your Paper and Bibliography") so that resources can be grouped on shorter sub-pages and not overwhelm students on the initial page they find (shown in figure 5.2), to arranging resources chronologically to cover the initial assignments first and then moving on to more complex assignments matched with a more complex

FIGURE 5.1 Embedded Librarian Page

niihka
Miami University Collaboration & Learning Environment
Beth Tumbleson (tumbleb) | Logout
My Workspace | PSY 221 M A | REL 101 M A | NSG 430 M A | BIS 401 V A | ECO 131 M A | More Sites | Exit Student View

Home
Announcements
Getting Started
Online Classroom
Forums
Assignments
Embedded Librarian
Tests & Quizzes
Gradebook
Search
Mail Sender
Schedule
Training and Support
Help
myMiami

Embedded Librarian

I am Beth Tumbleson, your Embedded Librarian

Assistant Director, Gardner-Harvey Library
Miami University Middletown, Middletown, Ohio 45042

E-mail me: **tumbleb@muohio.edu**
Call me: **513.727.3232**
Request a research consultation with me by filling out the online form.
Office Hours: Monday - Friday 8:30 AM to 5 PM and by appointment

As your embedded librarian I can assist you with

- **Selecting subject databases to find journal articles**
- **Search tips for databases, online catalogs, and search engines**
- **Finding electronic books for background information**
- **Using OhioLINK digital and print resources**
- **Citing sources**

The virtual Gardner-Harvey Library, Middletown is open 24/7. Start your course-related research at the Miami University Library Website!

Psychology Research Guide
Created by a Miami Librarian for students in psychology.

Working from Home?

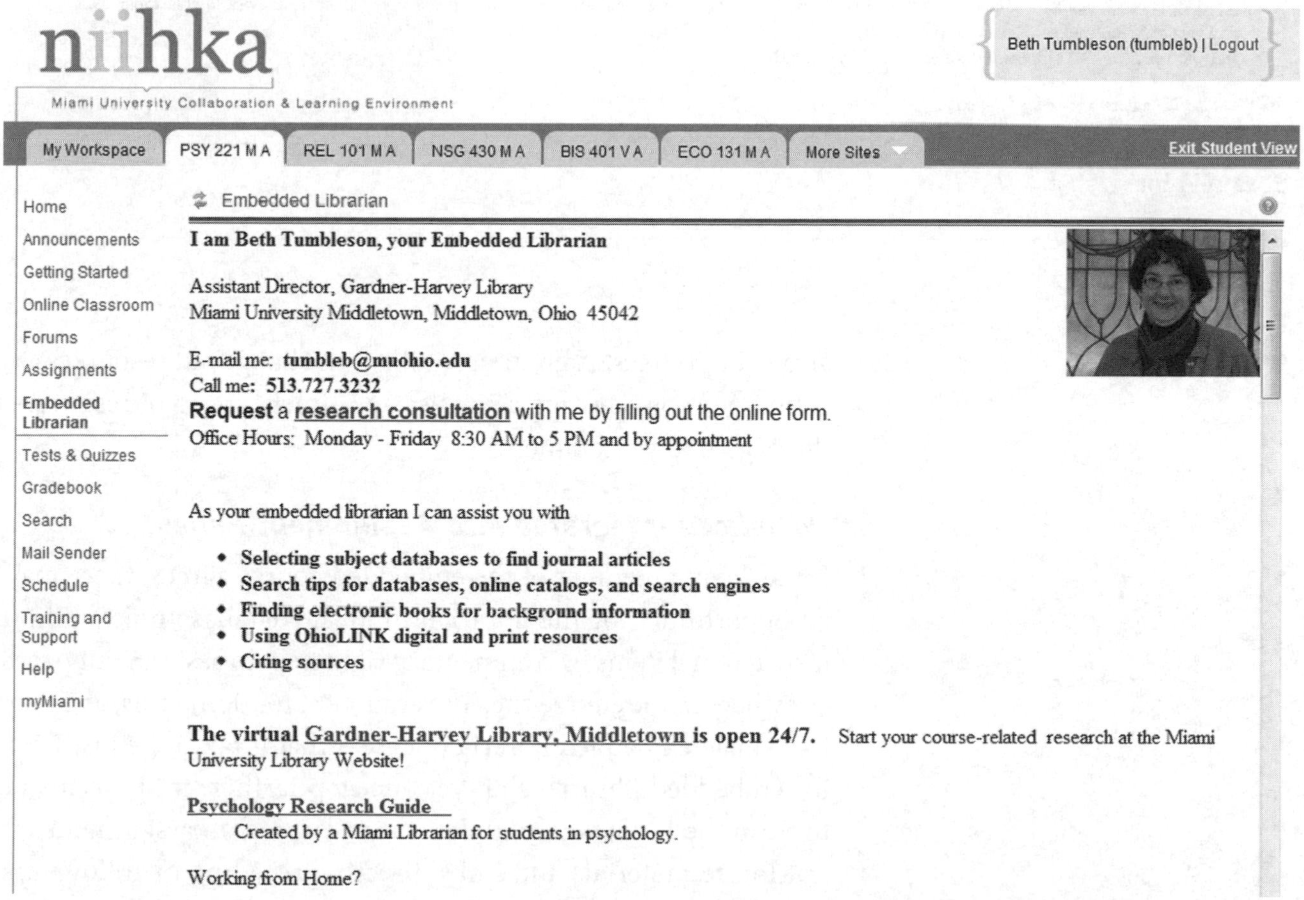

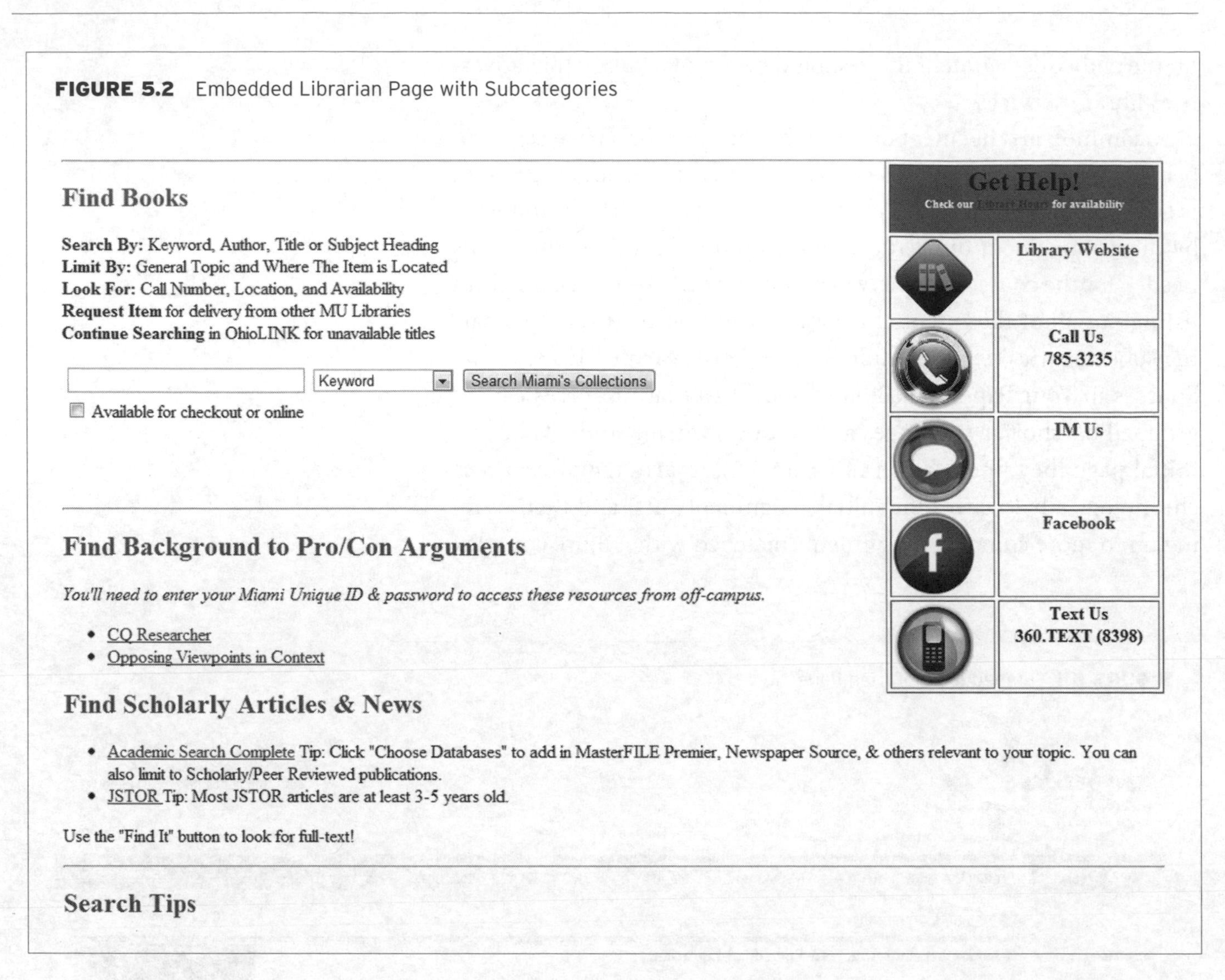

FIGURE 5.2 Embedded Librarian Page with Subcategories

array of resources. A librarian could even change out resources as the course goes on, keeping a concise and timely group of resources on the page at any one time.

Resources Integrated into Assignment Pages

If the faculty member of the embedded course agrees, there may be an opportunity for the librarian to locate database links and other instructional items or commentary right next to assignment pages or elsewhere in the course site. The argument for doing this, as opposed to a single embedded librarian page, is that it takes the justification for embedded librarianship yet one step farther: if librarians need to be in the LMS, where students are working on assignments, why not locate materials and links directly preceding or following the assignments themselves? Why make students hunt around for the embedded librarian page? There is no definitive evidence supporting one approach over the other, and some faculty may not be willing to share space in their pages for librarian content. But when possible, it does make sense to create as close a link as possible between the need for information and the resources to locate that information.

Sizing up the need for resources next to a given assignment or within a particular segment of course information is crucial. It would be overkill to repeat a lengthy list of resources everywhere that students might possibly need them. However, the ability to focus a small set of resources on a task at hand does allow that lengthy list to be intelligently divided throughout the course site. In figure 5.3, a segment of an instructor's page is shown that includes a few library resources linked at the point of need.

FIGURE 5.3 Embedded Library Resources Located Next to an Assignment

Add further to the evolving picture by doing some course-related research of your own. Your research efforts should take this direction. Identify a prominent public health leader(s) or group, whether nurse or other public health professional, who are currently addressing one of the problems the APHA has undertaken. **Be sure to explore the scholarly online databases suggested by the embedded librarian below to help you locate a modern day leader or group.**

Now prepare and post a three part answer to the Discussion Board based on your personal research and reflection on course readings and media. See questions below. You will compare a current day public health leader or group to such a public health reformer from the past. You must provide documented evidence for your discussion **by citing at least one source**: book, electronic book, electronic journal or newspaper article or authoritative Website. Use APA citation format to cite the source.

The Embedded Librarian Helps with Discussion Board 1. Beth Tumbleson
Based on assignment requirements, you will find these research strategies and library resources helpful to research leaders and topics in public health. Miami University Libraries makes available many electronic resources to use in academic research which are not free on the Internet.
To identify trustworthy public health organizations and issues, work from Websites you have evaluated as authoritative, accurate, current, comprehensive, and objective. This is essential in researching health issues and information. Always note the source of medical information!

Public Health Leaders of Today: Try a New Method of Research!
Who is your modern day public health hero? Anne Schuchat of the CDC? Dr. Paul Farmer, the subject of **Mountains Beyond Mountains?** Dr. Andrew Weil of **Why Our Health Matters?**

1.Biography in Context **(Miami ID & Password)**
Enter your Miami Unique ID and Password to access from off-campus. (Authentication is needed)
Click **Occupation** above the search box.
Enter: **nurse, nurse practicioner, nursing administrator, nursing educator, public health educator** or **public health nurse.**
Click **Search** and a list of names will appear.
Click a name to see information from **reference. news. and audio** sources.

Video Tutorials and Screencasts

It is one thing to link to databases on a page or write up some tips on using them; it is quite another to show students how to choose among them or perform sample searches in a video. There is much merit in creating short video tutorials or screencasts that will help students along in their research. Providing information visually can help students from a variety of learning styles understand the concepts or instructions given, especially those whose learning is strengthened by viewing diagrams or images related to what is being taught. These learning objects can also be watched multiple times by students to easily review material for clarity or to seek an answer to a specific need while searching. In situations where the opportunity for a face-to-face instruction session for students is impossible, tutorials or screenshots can provide a version of library instruction to students.

However, though videos are extremely useful, the time limits all librarians operate under requires prioritizing the creation of videos. Which content merits having a video dedicated to its explication? As will become clear below, there are several collections of existing videos and screencasts from which to draw. These learning object repositories are most useful for finding videos that explain the use of particular databases (which have common interfaces for all libraries that subscribe to them), or that cover generic information literacy concepts (citing sources, avoiding plagiarism, narrowing topics). The areas that seem most meaningful for creating your own video are explanations of how to move among your library's databases to research topics in the course, or how to navigate the library's website to find databases and library resources (as well as how to search the library's catalog), or how to work through a specific assignment. None of the preceding topics is likely to have been created by librarians at other institutions. These topics would be very helpful to students to understand how to use the resources they have at hand to complete the work in their course.

How can the embedded librarian go about creating videos or screencasts? There are several software options at hand for creating these materials. Adobe Captivate (figure 5.4) and TechSmith's Camtasia Studio are full fledged packages for capturing demonstrations of any activities that take place on-screen. They can both be used to mix the action occurring on the screen with screen-shot images, PowerPoint presentation slides, and short quiz questions that users must answer to proceed. In short, these software packages offer a range of services

Screencasting Tools

Adobe Captivate–
www.adobe.com/products/captivate.html

Screencast-O-Matic–
http://screencast-o-matic.com

Screenr–
www.screenr.com

TechSmith's Camtasia–
www.techsmith.com/camtasia.html

TechSmith's Jing–
www.techsmith.com/jing.html

Wikipedia comparison of screencasting tools–
http://en.wikipedia.org/wiki/Comparison_of_screencasting_software

FIGURE 5.4 Making a Tutorial In Adobe Captivate

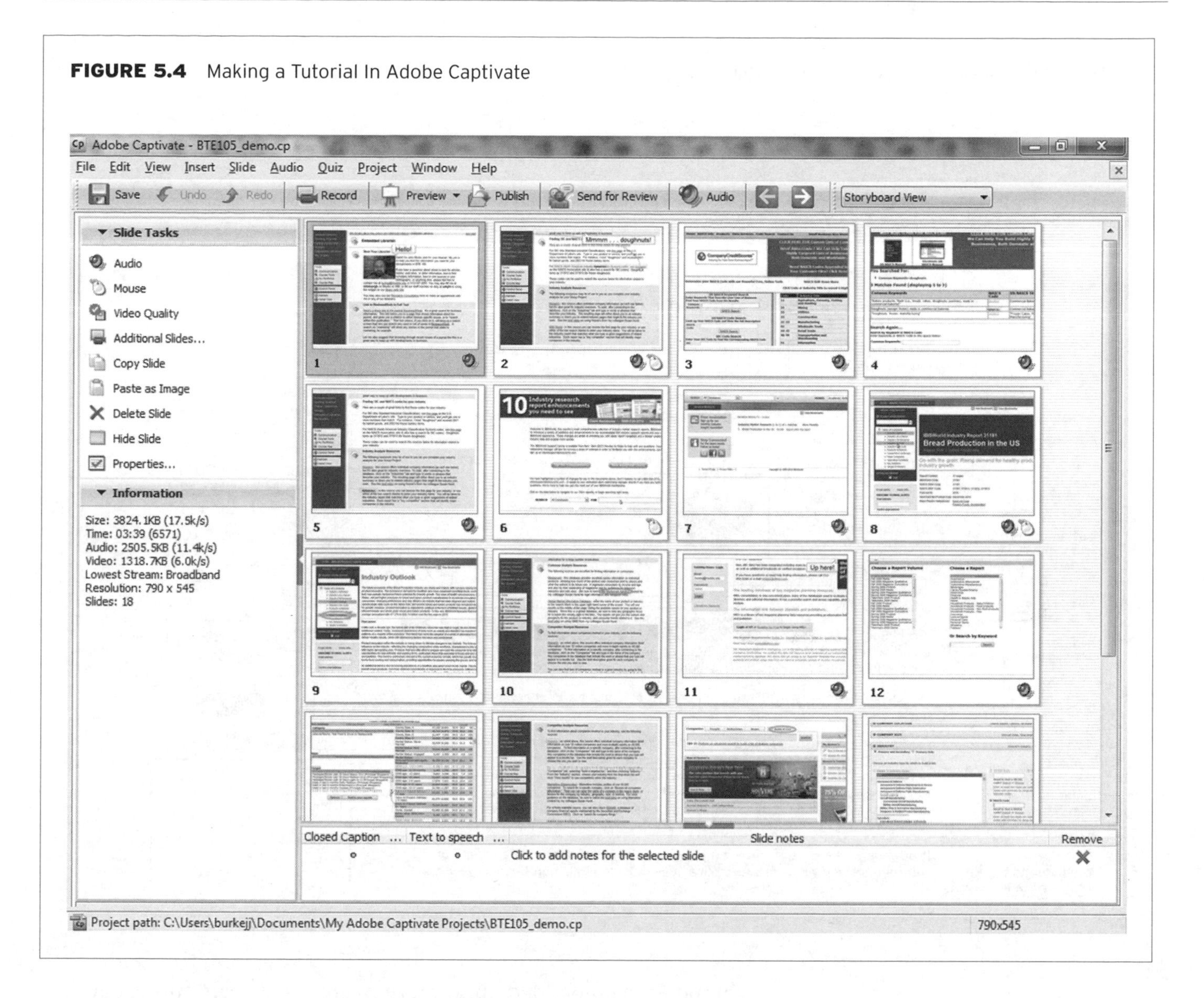

and options for a price. On the other hand, there are free versions of software available that allow for quick capture of screen activities. Jing from TechSmith, Screencast-O-Matic (figure 5.5), and Screenr are quite useful at creating a short demo or overview of moving through a website or database. Links to all of these tools and to a Wikipedia comparison of multiple screencasting tools are included in the sidebar.

Finding Existing Instructional Content

There are a number of collections of library-related learning objects that contain items that are usable in multiple library settings. Why

FIGURE 5.5 Making a Tutorial in Screencast-O-Matic

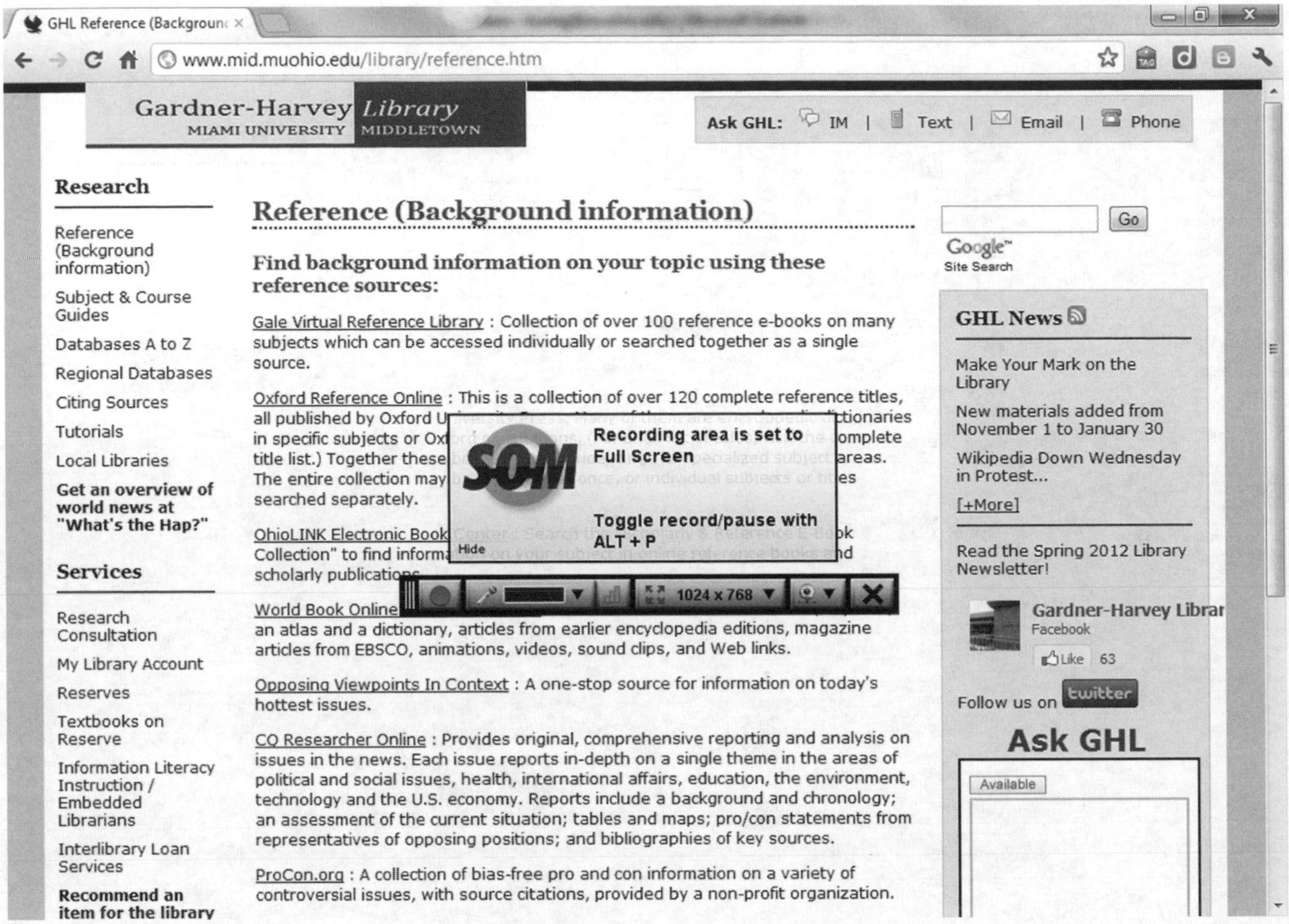

should each embedded librarian reinvent the wheel? This is particularly true of screencasts or video tutorials, but it also applies to other materials: step-by-step tutorials, quizzes, online handouts, exercises for students to complete, etc. A number of these items, in addition to screencasts, are found in collections of learning materials. They can also be located through Google searches (e.g., "library handout narrowing topic" or "library quiz evaluating sources") or, in the case of video content, by searching YouTube (www.youtube.com) by the topic of the content you desire (e.g., "avoiding plagiarism" or "scholarly vs. popular periodicals"). In addition to the highly useful collections listed in the sidebar, the authors also recommend the University of Illinois Libraries LibGuide on Learning Objects (http://uiuc.libguides.com/learningobjects), a tremendous guide to software on which to base learning objects, and also a great guide to collections of online instructional material. All of these resources can be helpful in finding content to add to an embedded course that fills instructional gaps beyond what the embedded librarian can create and supply.

Finding Your Voice: Approaching Online Writing

Another word is needed about the use of words. As you are creating your embedded librarian pages of links and screencasts and handouts (oh my!), it is easy to let the love of language get away from you. However, excessive verbiage on a page can obscure the very important guidance, links, or strategic advice you mean to provide. Students who view an embedded librarian page with paragraphs of narrative may decide it is not worth reading through to get to the good stuff. Or too much "library-ese" may lose your users' attention when it is most needed. These and other errors can be avoided, however.

The key is to think about what you write from the perspective of your audience. Resist the desire to tell everything. Be mindful of how easily readers will be able to understand the content you have created and move through the tasks before them. Evaluate the entire scope of the pieces you have put together, following your design for the embedded materials, to make sure the whole document or set of documents are understandable and easy to move through and between. Some excellent advice in this direction appears in Redish (2007), including the following items from her 10 guidelines for improving sentences in web content:

- Talk to your site visitors. Use "you."
- Write in the active voice (most of the time).
- Write short, simple, straightforward sentences.
- Give extra information its own place.
- Start with the context—first things first, second things second.

Collections of Library Instructional Content

ANTS (ANimated Tutorial Sharing) Project–
www.screencast.com/users/ANTS

CLIP (Cooperative Library Instruction Project)–
www.clipinfolit.org/tutorials

LION (Library Information literacy Online Network)–
http://blip.tv/LIONTV

MERLOT (Multimedia Educational Resource for Learning and Online Teaching)–
www.merlot.org (look under the Library and Information Services category)

PRIMO (Peer-Reviewed Instructional Materials Online) Database–
www.ala.org/apps/primo/public/search.cfm

Implementation

The Implementation phase is all about putting the materials you have developed into place. This should flow naturally, given that you have spent time designing what should go into the embedded classroom and then developing content to fit that design. Any necessary last-minute training in using the LMS should be accomplished so that the documents, links, screencasts, and other materials can be added. After all of the hard work in preparing the embedded librarian presence, it is time to put everything in place.

One consideration that is worth noting before implementation begins is the issue of time. Does everything you have developed need to be in place on the opening day of the semester? Not at all. In fact, some materials may be better moved in place on a gradual basis as the course progresses and new assignments necessitate new content. This is true of both text and link content, but it may also involve the embedded librarian's participation in discussion boards or forums. There can be a more staged, or growing, involvement in the course by the librarian as the course calendar turns toward more research-heavy assignments. A certain amount of material should be present at the beginning of any course (e.g., librarian contact information), and then other items can be added in as needed.

Layout of Materials

Following on the discussion above of how the embedded librarian content will be placed in the LMS, the Implementation phase is the point to make final decisions on layout. Again, there should be at least some information on the library and its resources that is readily available from the student's point of entry into the course site. Beyond that, though, it is certainly possible to locate key resources within the instructor's provided content and assignments. This last option requires some coordination with the faculty member so that the librarian's material is placed in a timely manner. In addition to the text and link content, there are also screencasts or videos to consider. One consideration is whether those items will be located in the embedded librarian page (or other course pages), or just linked to on those pages. If video files are embedded, the video may be watched right on that page. This also makes the screencast or video stand out on the page. Finally, the librarian must decide on how she will monitor discussion boards or forums in the LMS. This may be done through reading through instructor- or student-created topics within the discussion board or forum, or by creating a separate topic (or multiple topics) dedicated to questions asked of the embedded librarian. Some of these decisions can be made earlier during the Development phase, but there is always an opportunity to fine tune the layout of content when implementing your materials.

Evaluation

It is not enough for the embedded librarian to place the materials in the course; the time comes to see how, and how well, students are using the resources. The question of assessment in embedded librarianship will be dealt with more fully in chapter 7, but a word on evaluation is quite useful here to wrap up the ADDIE process. As Strickland (2012) notes, there are two kinds of evaluation to practice here: formative and summative. Formative evaluation can be conducted as the course is ongoing to help address barriers or problems that students encounter, and summative evaluation is done at the conclusion of the course to see if learning goals have been met.

Formative Evaluation

Methods of formative evaluation are perhaps more difficult to implement for the embedded librarian, since the course is continuing during the evaluation period. Because students and faculty are focused on completing the course assignments and achieving the larger course instructional goals, they may be less willing or able to comment upon their use of library resources (or, in the case of faculty, their observations of students' use). But conversations with faculty following research assignments may help the embedded librarian recognize gaps in or continuing needs for library instruction based on students' performance on assignments. It may be possible to get reactions from a small number of students in the class, perhaps through direct e-mails or a short web survey. Farmer (2011) has an excellent discussion of assessment measures and choosing among them for the purposes of evaluating instructional activities. The goal of formative assessment or evaluation is to change what the embedded librarian offers to improve her services to students for the remainder of the course.

Summative Evaluation

Summative evaluation at the end of the course can be helpful to give the embedded librarian an overall view of how her efforts impacted students in the course. This evaluation can be accomplished through a variety of methods as outlined by Farmer (2011), including web surveys of students' and faculty members' impressions of the embedded librarian's participation, pre- and post-testing of students' information literacy skills, and assessment of assignments. The goal here is to understand what worked and what did not for the entirety of the course, with the aim of improving future offerings.

Summary

With careful attention to setting goals and creating helpful course content, the embedded librarian can design an effective instructional approach to teach students research skills within the larger course. Using an instructional design process such as ADDIE, the embedded librarian can analyze the course to identify students' needs, design content that will address them, develop useful learning objects (or find ones created by others), implement them, and then evaluate the process. The process discussed in the chapter should guide the embedded librarian through each course in which she is embedded.

References

Bell, Steven J., and John D. Shank. 2007. *Academic Librarianship by Design: A Blended Librarian's Guide to the Tools and Techniques*. Chicago: American Library Association.

Farmer, Leslie S. J. 2011. *Instructional Design for Librarians and Information Professionals*. New York: Neal-Schuman Publishers, Inc.

Redish, Janice (Ginny). 2007. *Letting Go of the Words: Writing Web Content that Works*. San Francisco: Morgan Kaufmann Publishers.

Strickland, A. W. (n.d.) "ADDIE." Idaho State University College of Education, Science, Math and Technology Education. http://ed.isu.edu/addie/index.html.

Online, Face-to-Face, and Hybrid Courses

Introduction

IN THIS CHAPTER:

One false expectation of embedded librarianship is that it only works, or works best, in supporting online courses. Though much development and practice of embedded librarianship is focused on online courses, and is necessarily located in an online environment (the LMS), this is not the only arena in which embedded librarianship is an effective service. The concept that embedded librarianship positions librarians in the right spot to impact students' research work is applicable to all types of classes that use an LMS: face-to-face, fully online, or hybrid. There are differences in how embedded services are extended to each of those types, but embedded librarianship can succeed in all three.

To give some context for how embedded librarians are working with these different types of classes, the authors' survey of embedded librarians (see appendix) asked respondents to indicate whether or not they worked with each type. Here are the results from the 280 respondents, showing the number who chose each response and the percentage of total responses (respondents were encouraged to choose more than one option where applicable):

- Traditional, on-site face-to-face courses (181)—69 percent
- Online or web-based courses (183)—70 percent
- Hybrid courses (taught part face-to-face and part online) (140)—53 percent

All three types are quite common among the authors' sample (a fourth variation, off-site face-to-face courses, taught off of the institution's campus, was chosen by 50 respondents [19 percent]. There may be institutions that only offer online courses, and therefore can only embed in that type, or institutions that offer only face-to-face or hybrid courses and are limited in embedded librarianship options as well. But a reasonable guess is that most responding institutions offer a blend of online, face-to-face, and hybrid courses, and are applying their embedded model to at least two of these types.

This chapter will explore special needs and considerations for embedding library services in each type of course. Examples will be shared to help you imagine how embedded librarianship may differ in each situation.

Online Learning Courses

Online courses are a significant portion of higher education enrollment. Allen and Seaman (2011) surveyed over 2,500 educational institutions, and found that 31 percent of students are taking one or more online classes. In an online course, the expectation is that course materials will all be provided through the means of presenting the course (usually web-based in some way, generally through an LMS). There will likely be a mix of synchronous and asynchronous instruction methods along with the opportunity for both of these types of communication among groups of students or students and the instructor. Students in the courses may be located within a close geographical area or can be spread around the world. They may have chosen the course because it is more convenient for their schedules (especially in an asynchronous course), they may enjoy this method of learning, or they may be limited to taking the course through this format (say, in a program that is only offered online, or because of the students' distance from the institution). Students may have the technological skills to navigate web-based resources easily, but that is not an absolute given. Similarly, students may be technologically aware, but those skills may not automatically transfer to information-seeking and assessment tasks, which may be new ground for the students.

The cozy confines of the online course can include different elements. In a more asynchronous mode, course readings and recorded lectures are linked within the course site for students to experience over the course of the class (perhaps arranged in module folders, one per week of the course). Students complete assignments electronically and submit them to a drop box within the course site. Interaction among students or between individual students and the instructor occur through a discussion board or forum, through individual or course-wide blogs, via e-mail, or through a synchronous chat tool.

In a more synchronous mode, the instructor may use web conferencing or collaboration tools to share real-time lectures with students, allowing students to post questions via chat during the presentation. Students may work in groups on projects using the same collaboration tool. As with the asynchronous model, course readings and assignments are also posted in the course site and turned in there.

How does the web-based delivery of the course impact the embedded librarian's work with the class? All of the LMS tools used by the instructor or students are available to the librarian as well. An embedded librarian can post resources and instructional information within the course site, and can also use the same tools that instructors use for lectures, either synchronous or asynchronous, to hold an instructional session with the class. There may be a greater need to use screencasts to pass on instructional guidance on the use of databases. There may also be a need to monitor discussion boards/forums or blogs more closely to pick up on student research needs or to address any difficulties students may have experienced. In general, the embedded librarian must imagine that all interactions with the class will take place within the LMS or in using other online tools.

Konieczny (2011) presents an example of embedded library services in online courses offered at Ferris State University. There, librarians are embedded in several online courses in the Master of Science in Nursing (MSN) program and in the Health Care Systems Administration (HCSA) program. There is extensive use of the discussion board in the HCSA courses for posting weekly article research assignment responses, and the embedded librarians assist in this task. An online folder of library resources (database links, etc.) is posted in each course for students to refer to, and then librarians check with students to see if they have difficulties posting the required articles. Web-conferencing software allows the librarians to hold information literacy sessions in real-time with the classes, sharing their desktops to demonstrate databases and search approaches. Students can ask questions using the chat feature.

Online Courses and Embedded Librarians

Upsides

- Students are in the LMS for all coursework.
- Opportunities for synchronous instruction with the whole class may exist.

Downsides

- May require more in-depth tutorials and instructional materials than a face-to-face course.
- Increases need to monitor online discussions and offer research assistance.

Opportunities

- Can reach higher percentage of students due to increased use of LMS.
- Can test and apply multiple Web 2.0 tools and LMS tools to an all-online environment.

Face-to-Face Courses

Face-to-face courses follow the traditional model of teaching students in a classroom or lab. The Campus Computing Project's 2011 survey found that 59 percent of all college and university courses use an LMS. So, even removing online and hybrid courses from the mix leaves a significant number of face-to-face courses that have some involvement with the LMS. Instructors of these courses may at least post their syllabi or use the gradebook tool in their LMS. Others will use a wider array of tools, including broader document posting, online discussions, and perhaps synchronous communications through chat or web conferencing outside of normal class meeting times.

With face-to-face courses, the approach to embedded librarianship has a bit more flexibility than with online courses, because the students and instructor are meeting in real-time. Face-to-face courses that utilize an embedded librarian tend to make more than brief use of the LMS within the course. The LMS may house copies of the syllabus and other course documents, assignment information (and also an assignment drop box), course readings, and other materials. The expectation is that instruction in the physical classroom will be supplemented by students using the LMS to access the materials above. Much of the librarian's implementation of library resources and instructional materials in the course's LMS site will be similar to the approach used with online courses, but there is an important difference.

Since face-to-face courses have regular class meetings, the librarian can utilize real-time interactions with students in addition to LMS-based services. This lets the embedded librarian hold one or more library instruction sessions with the class to allow for hands-on instruction in a computer lab or the chance to demonstrate resources and take questions from students. Depending on the needs of the students and the wishes of the instructor, the librarian could make a brief visit to introduce herself as the embedded librarian and give a short overview of what this means, and then return at an appropriate time to offer a lengthier session. Embedded librarianship offers many improvements on other modes of library instruction, but it does not require that those modes be left behind. Face-to-face instruction with a class can provide a valuable way to share information that is also provided inside in the course site.

If the distance is not too great, a real-time library instruction session can be held for a face-to-face course held at a site other than the institution's campus. Off-campus face-to-face courses can be addressed more as online courses from the standpoint of connecting with and instructing the class if traveling to the site is impossible. But if a visit is possible, then the experience of embedding in the class may not be much different from embedding in other face-to-face classes on campus.

At Marshall University, an intensive program of face-to-face library instruction with courses was shown to be ineffective in advancing students' research skills and knowledge. An initial response was to create a set of online modules, including screencasts and tutorials, which could be used in the LMS with multiple course sections. Embedded librarians then created a new embedded model so that more individualized course materials could be developed and implemented by embedded librarians in each course. The librarians were able to increase the number of times that students were learning about library-related skills to go beyond the one-shot model. Librarians collaborated with course faculty to choose the most opportune times to provide course-specific sessions to communicate the essential resources needed in the course (Bean and Thomas 2010).

Hybrid or Blended Courses

Hybrid or blended courses combine elements of online and face-to-face models. They provide the ability to provide instruction face-to-face for part of the duration of the course and then through asynchronous or synchronous means in the LMS for the rest of the time. This division of class contact time between the two models helps make the hybrid course more flexible for students and faculty, and can also help compress the time required to complete the course (e.g., a course normally held over a 15-week semester may be offered in hybrid form over an eight-week period). The provision of materials in the LMS and the ability for online discussion make the time away from the classroom function well for learning course content.

In this environment, there are natural points for the embedded librarian to assist students in a hybrid course. There is the ability to meet with the course as needed for face-to-face instruction in

Face-to-Face Courses and Embedded Librarians

Upsides

- Can appear in face-to-face classroom in addition to embedding in the LMS.
- Could offer multiple short sessions (rather than one full-class session) to better fit research needs of the moment.

Downsides

- Need to remember to make use of LMS for longer contact with the class.
- Have to fine-tune amount of resources linked in the LMS to match with face-to-face instruction (avoid overkill).

Opportunities

- Can possibly conduct real-time instruction sessions with off-campus face-to-face courses.
- Chance for a balanced approach between hands-on instruction and online contact with students.

addition to all of the opportunities available to work with students and share information through the LMS. Hybrid courses can be imagined as potentially the best of both worlds for students, faculty, and librarians. As this type of course becomes more prevalent, there will be more ways to approach embedding library services.

Hybrid or Blended Courses and Embedded Librarians

Upside

- The librarian can work with the faculty member to figure out which information literacy concepts are best to introduce online and which are better in face-to-face classroom.

Downside

- Depending on how the hybrid course is conducted, the librarian's experience may be more like that in an online course or more like a face-to-face course.

Opportunity

- The librarian can choose among methods already used with both online and face-to-face courses.

Interactivity with Students

Left purposefully unmentioned in the above descriptions of embedding librarians in the various course types is how those librarians will be able to communicate and interact directly with students. It is easy to imagine the audiences for each type of course falling into distinct groups with differing access options for the librarian to use. But it is not as simple as expecting that face-to-face course students will be able to interact with embedded librarians in person, nor that online or hybrid students will prefer or be restricted to virtual communication methods. Depending on the student groups involved, librarians may find that they will use all possible communication means in the course of interacting with their classes.

In the authors' institution, a very close network of university campuses and off-site locations makes for a large community of students who are taking multiple course types (in multiple locations) at once. With a maximum of an hour's drive from location to location, it is feasible to have students taking face-to-face courses on more than one campus or off-campus site at once, perhaps in addition to an online course. This means that students will use the various virtual means of communication to ask questions, but will also be able to drop by the campus library or make an appointment for a research consultation with their embedded librarian. Librarians within the institution travel to off-campus sites for instruction sessions, gaining that face-to-face contact with classes, and those same students may travel to the campus for research assistance. Online courses offered by the institution do have students who live far from any of the campuses, but also have substantial numbers of students who may be on the same campus as the instructor. Another facet of this arrangement is that two of the university campuses are commuter campuses, and students in face-to-face courses with busy lives and responsibilities beyond the campus may not be able to stop by the library, but would rather interact through e-mail or instant messaging.

TABLE 6.1 Methods for Interacting with Students in Each Course Type

	Online	Face-to-Face	Hybrid or Blended
In library	Maybe	Yes	Yes
Research consultation	Maybe	Yes	Yes
E-mail	Yes	Yes	Yes
Instant messaging	Yes	Yes	Yes
Texting	Yes	Yes	Yes
Web conferencing and collaboration tools	Yes	Maybe	Yes

So, when planning to interact with students, it pays to have the most options available. Inviting students to e-mail, chat or instant message, text the library, use web conferencing or collaboration tools, and make in-person research consultation appointments will cover multiple situations. Table 6.1 outlines these options and connects them to the various types of courses in which they may be used. These may be offered by utilizing tools within the LMS or by using the various communication methods that the library offers to all students (whether or not they are participating in embedded courses). It makes sense to cast the net widely for research needs and then adjust the embedded librarian's offerings as students respond (or not). Again, situations and environments will differ, and there may be easier lines to draw with some student groups than with others, but flexibility should be sought in embedded library services.

Summary

Embedded librarianship is a flexible method for collaborating with faculty and connecting with students, no matter what type of course is involved. Librarians can work in face-to-face, online, and hybrid or blended courses, taking note of some necessary adjustments for each type. As the authors' survey shows, embedded librarians are already pursuing multiple course types with their services.

References

Allen, I. Elaine, and Jeff Seaman. 2011. "Going the Distance: Online Education in the USA 2011." Babson Survey Research Group. www.onlinelearningsurvey.com/reports/goingthedistance.pdf.

Bean, Teresa M., and Sabrina N. Thomas. 2010. "Being Like Both: Library Instruction Methods that Outshine the One-Shot." *Public Services Quarterly* 6 (2/3): 237–249.

Campus Computing Project. 2011. "2011 National Survey of Information Technology in U.S. Higher Education." www.campuscomputing.net/sites/www.campuscomputing.net/files/Green-CampusComputing2011_2.pdf.

Konieczny, Alison. 2010. "Experiences as an Embedded Librarian in Online Courses." *Medical Reference Services Quarterly* 29 (1): 47–57.

Assessing the Impact of Embedded Librarians

Introduction

Evaluation, as addressed in chapter 5, is the key final step of the instructional design process, helping to improve and fine-tune a method of teaching content to students. The process can then begin anew to refine instruction and build new instructional content and tools. As the ADDIE model has been applied to embedded librarianship, it is part of the work of librarians to assess their efforts. Assessment is rarely a task that anyone looks forward to, but there are some motivational reasons for pursuing it. Measuring the work and effectiveness of embedded librarians will give each librarian and each embedded librarian program directions for further growth and a clearer sense of what has been, and is yet to be, accomplished in each setting. In aggregate form, assessment helps the body of embedded librarians justify their efforts and helps other librarians decide whether or not to join in.

When designing a plan of assessment, there are several questions to be answered. Matthews (2007) suggests four questions that will shape the outcome of assessment:

- What is the purpose of the assessment?
- Who is the audience for the assessment?
- What will the assessment focus on?
- What resources are available for assessment?

This chapter is designed to examine these four questions. The purpose has been dealt with in part already in this introduction, and the audience is clearly students, faculty, and librarians who participate

IN THIS CHAPTER:

in embedded library services. But the focus or foci of the assessment work and the resources and methods that can be used will be discussed in more detail. The main goal for any embedded library program is to establish some sort of ongoing assessment process to help measure its utility.

In the authors' survey of embedded librarians (see appendix), respondents were asked how they assess their embedded librarianship efforts. From the choices offered, the respondents provided the following results:

- Surveys of participating students (102)—48 percent
- Other (86)—40 percent
- Surveys of participating faculty (70)—33 percent
- Analysis of student research assignments (51)—24 percent
- Information literacy assessments of students (pre- and post-tests) (43)—20 percent
- Focus groups of participating students (11)—5 percent
- Focus groups of participating faculty (10)—5 percent

Surveys are clearly the most popular method of assessment, for both students and faculty. The "Other" category responses largely consisted of statements that no formal assessment program was yet in place for the embedded librarian program (in some cases because the program had just started). In addition, some respondents used the "Other" category to note that their current assessment may involve one of the defined measures above in addition to word-of-mouth feedback from students and/or faculty. Notable in the results is that nearly a quarter of respondents are examining student work to assess the impact of embedded librarianship. A fifth of the librarians administer pre- and post-tests of students' information literacy skills. Judging from the survey results and the literature, librarians are working hard to develop and implement methods of assessment. This chapter will examine that work, considering options available and providing an overview of the results to date.

The Focus of Your Assessment

Before heading into an examination of the methods used for assessment, it is useful to think about what you hope to learn from the endeavor. The Introduction covered some reasons to gather this information from a design process perspective (continuous improvement of instructional offerings) and from the perspective of justifying embedded librarianship (testing the premises of this mode of instruction and interaction to see if they hold up). These are important purposes to include in your assessment design, but they are also rather broad purposes until they are further defined. As you venture into choosing your methods of assessment, it is time to consider what specific questions you hope to answer.

Perhaps you are interested in assessing your design choices about where to place materials within the embedded course site (next to the assignment, among the course content, on a separate embedded librarian page, etc.). Maybe your focus is on figuring out which communication methods students prefer when receiving updates or suggestions from the embedded librarian, or on how well faculty members believe that embedded librarians are accomplishing the goals they set together for students' research skills. You may also want to test how much (if at all) students have improved their abilities to perform information literacy skills during the course of their work with an embedded librarian. All of these questions will lead to the development of more specific questions to gather information toward fulfilling the focus of your assessment. But assessment is not a one-size-fits-all proposition. The precise method or methods that you use will depend on what you and your colleagues wish to learn.

Since you are working with your library colleagues to design, develop, and implement embedded library services at your institution, you will have excellent insights into decisions you have made and questions that have arisen. You can start developing questions and choosing your purposes by brainstorming with colleagues and reflecting on your experiences with interacting with students and faculty members. You will want to go beyond this circle to look at what other embedded librarians have devised for assessment (more examples of this will follow). It would also be useful to consult with faculty members in whose courses you embed and see what they would like to learn about their students' experiences. You are not alone in this process.

Assessment Methods

Now it is time to turn to the methods embedded librarians can use to assess their efforts. The options listed below are not meant as an exhaustive list of techniques or a lengthy catalog of examples, but rather a suggested list of methods to draw on as you design your assessment plan. They represent options to consider when choosing the best method or methods to address the questions you have chosen to assess. Table 7.1 can be helpful in considering the methods in terms of their audiences, what they assess, when they can be used, and how the embedded librarian can use the feedback provided.

Depending on what you hope to learn from assessment, you may need to use multiple methods. Or there may be a single method used routinely with other methods brought in on occasion to investigate

TABLE 7.1 Methods of Assessment Summary

Method	Audience	What Is Being Assessed	Timing	What the Embedded Librarian Can Do with the Feedback
Surveys	Students/Faculty	Perceptions and self-reported use of the service	After class	Shape future embedded librarian offerings with feedback on use, impressions, and suggestions for improvement
Focus Groups	Students/Faculty	Perceptions of the service; suggestions for improvement	Before/after class	Shape future embedded librarian offerings with feedback on use, impressions, and suggestions for improvement
Information Literacy Assessments	Students	Student performance on information literacy tasks	Pre- and post-test	See impact of embedded librarianship on changing student performance
Assignment Analysis	Students	Student performance of research skills	After class	Assess the real-world application of information literacy skills by students
LMS Statistics	Students	Student activity with embedded librarian materials	After/during class	Tell which materials were viewed by students and how often
Usability Testing	Students	The design of the embedded librarian materials	Prior to class	Redesign the instructional materials

newly arisen questions. For instance, there may be a regular survey evaluation conducted at the conclusion of each semester in all embedded courses. Then, in order to assess newly added database tutorials, a librarian might also conduct a focus group of students and faculty to see how the tutorials were used and how they could be improved. It is certainly possible to over-assess a library service, but there are times when an additional measure can add useful data or perceptions—and not just end up as so much navel gazing.

Surveys of Students and Faculty

Students are the key audience for embedded library services and an excellent resource for input when asked how they perceive the service. A student survey can be used in multiple ways and at multiple points in the course of the class—perhaps in a short form in the midst of the course to check understanding. At the very least it can serve as an evaluation of the embedded librarian's work at the conclusion of the semester. Faculty members are likewise a great source of input on the conduct of the service. They can comment on the impact that the service has had on their students' research skills, shown through the works that students create from their research.

Since embedded librarianship in the LMS is focused on the online environment, it is natural to use web-based survey tools to gather data. The exam or quiz tools within the LMS provide a possible option for creating a survey that is located in the same environment that students use for other tests. Other survey tools may be available through the librarian's institution or from commercial services like SurveyMonkey (www.surveymonkey.com) or Zoomerang (www.zoomerang.com). Those tools are free for short surveys of 10 questions or fewer. Another excellent free option is available from Google Docs (http://docs.google.com), which has a survey form option that is easy to set up. All of these options will allow you to accept anonymous responses from those you survey. Note that you may need to check with your institution's institutional review board (IRB) before pursuing a survey, but generally surveys used for program improvement (and not wider research) will be allowed by the IRB without an additional proposal.

The length of the survey may vary from library to library, but a shorter survey tends to motivate more respondents to complete it. Questions can be formed based on the areas of focus for your assessment. Areas of importance will likely include whether students used the service, did they find it helpful, did they learn about new resources or strategies, and so forth. For faculty, there could also be questions on whether they would use the service again and whether students learned the information literacy skills that the librarian and faculty member intended them to. It is useful to include an open answer section on the survey so that respondents can comment on aspects of the service that they thought were useful or that were in need of adjustment. Open comments can be hard to classify and enumerate in survey results, but they can reveal issues or benefits that do not occur to the librarians creating the survey. For instance, an open answer response noting that the embedded librarian should have announced her presence in the class earlier than she did can cause helpful reflection on how communicating the service to students could be improved.

This is just a beginning of advice on creating surveys; for more information see Westbrook (2001) for guidance on question and survey design. For one approach to survey questions, see a sample embedded library survey for students in figure 7.1 and one for faculty members in figure 7.2. Samples of these surveys are also available at www.users.muohio.edu/burkejj/embeddedsurveys.html.

Focus Groups

This method can be used with either students or faculty or a combination of both groups. Focus groups are moderated discussions on aspects of embedded library services, generally by groups of six to 12 people (Westbrook 2001). The participants are asked a list of open-ended questions by a facilitator who encourages group members to participate and follow up on the thoughts expressed. Groups will meet for around an hour, or perhaps longer if more time is needed to cover the required questions. For instance, a group of students who took part in courses with embedded librarians could gather to discuss how they used the embedded librarian service. Questions might include:

- How did you search for information when working on assignments in your course?
- What are one or two things the embedded librarian could do to make your research work better?
- Where did you find the best information for your work in the course?

FIGURE 7.1 Example of Student Web Survey

Embedded Librarian Survey

Thank you for participating in the Embedded Librarian survey! Your responses will help us evaluate the program for this semester and improve our embedded librarian service for the future. Please answer as many questions as are applicable to your experience with the embedded librarian program. All responses to the survey are anonymous, except for any identifying information you may enter in the open text box at the end. We appreciate you taking the time to fill this out.

*1. Choose the class number and section code for your class that had an embedded librarian.

Select:

2. During the semester, did you click on and use any of the posted links or research strategies placed in your Niihka course site by the embedded librarian?

- Yes
- No

3. Were any of the research databases, e-books, or websites provided by the embedded librarian new to you?

- Yes
- No

*4. Where and how in your Niihka course site would you like research help posted (links to databases, citing sources information, search terms, etc.)? Rank the following choices in the order that you would use them, with 1 being the most likely choice and 4 being the least likely choice.

	*				
	1	2	3	4	N/A
Next to an instructor-posted assignment	◯	◯	◯	◯	◯
On a separate embedded librarian page in the classroom	◯	◯	◯	◯	◯
In a Niihka Forum	◯	◯	◯	◯	◯
Emailed directly to you	◯	◯	◯	◯	◯

- If you could improve one thing about your experience with finding information for the course, what would it be?

The focus group experience can add some depth to the results of a broader survey. You are not able to capture the thoughts of as large a group as with a survey, but you can explore responses much further than in the survey model. Imagine reading a response to a survey question and wanting to ask "why?" to the respondent, who now cannot be reached (due to anonymity). With the focus group, that follow-up is possible, and adds dimension to the response. The focus group method could be used for assessment of completed embedded librarian work, or it could be very helpful in shaping the start of a new service.

FIGURE 7.2 Example of Faculty Web Survey

MIAMI UNIVERSITY MIDDLETOWN
Gardner-Harvey Library

Embedded Librarian Survey

Thank you for participating in the Embedded Librarian survey! Your responses will help us evaluate and improve our embedded librarian service for the coming semester. Please answer as many questions as are applicable to your experience with the embedded librarian program. All responses to the survey are anonymous, except for any identifying information you may enter in the open text box at the end. We appreciate you taking the time to fill this out.

1. The embedded librarian introduced students to course-specific library resources for research which were new to them.

Strongly disagree | | Neutral | | Strongly agree
1 | 2 | 3 | 4 | 5

2. The embedded librarian provided useful tutorials, tools, and instruction on the research process.

Strongly disagree | | Neutral | | Strongly agree
1 | 2 | 3 | 4 | 5

3. The participation of the embedded librarian in my course impacted the design of my research assignments and my research assignment handouts.

Strongly disagree | | Neutral | | Strongly agree
1 | 2 | 3 | 4 | 5

Information Literacy Assessments of Students

Another possible method for assessment is to test students' abilities to perform information literacy tasks or show their knowledge of library terms and skills. This can be done using a formal or commercial test product, or through a locally-created quiz or set of exercises (see the sidebar for a list of possible options). The main idea is to have a way to show that students' abilities have improved due to the work of the embedded librarian. The difficulty comes in isolating which factors have actually changed students' performance and in showing a change in their performance over a fairly short period of time. This need to isolate drives assessment toward a focus on information literacy skills that tend to be taught primarily by the embedded librarian.

Testing can be done at various times in the course. It can be completed at the end of the course, at the conclusion of a face-to-face or online instruction session, at any logical spot in the semester, or in a pre- and post-test comparative mode at either end of the semester. The most meaningful approach would be to have a comparison of students' abilities before they were involved with the research activities and information literacy instruction within the course. A well-designed test can show the improvement in students' competencies between the beginning of the course (the pre-test) and once they have learned the content and skills they encounter in the course. Generally, it is best to give the same test on both occasions to more clearly show the change between the two time periods.

The main difficulty with this testing approach (whether involving pre- and post-tests or not) is that it does take time. The length of the assessment can vary, but some portion of a class meeting time will be needed to administer the test in a face-to-face course. Students in these courses may not make time to complete a web-based test outside of class, so this is the only way to guarantee a captive audience of participating students. An online or hybrid course poses fewer constraints of time (perhaps), but students may not cooperate in this situation either. The faculty member can strongly influence the testing experience for good or ill. She may be happy to provide an incentive to students for taking the test (e.g., course extra credit). On the other hand, the faculty member may not be willing to cede instructional time to the librarian for an assessment test. The barriers of motivation and participation are not insurmountable, but they can make testing a less appealing option.

Information Literacy Assessments

- Educational Testing Service iSkills Assessment—www.ets.org/iskills
- Project SAILS (Standardized Assessment of Information Literacy Skills)—www.projectsails.org
- TRAILS (Tool for Real-time Assessment of Information Literacy Skills)—www.trails-9.org
- WASSAIL (Web-based Augustana Student Survey Assessment of Information Literacy—www.library.ualberta.ca/augustana/infolit/wassail

Analysis of Student Research Assignments

If you have ever been curious to know which resources students actually end up using in their papers, this assessment method is for you. This approach gives the librarian an opportunity to view the results of one or more assignments from the class in order to assess how well students pursued their research. It can be as simple as noting whether students met the minimum criteria for the assignment (i.e., three scholarly journal articles and six citations overall) or noting whether students used the suggested databases or other finding tools to locate the sources in their works cited list. The more difficult end of this might involve assessing the fit of the chosen sources to a student's topic or judging whether the sources provide a good balance of information sources. The librarian can create a rubric or set of expectations for assessing each assignment, which can be based on the instructor's requirements for the bibliography and sources for the assignment. The RAILS (Rubric Assessment of Information Literacy Skills) project has a tremendous number of rubrics that could be models for this sort of assessment (see them at www.railsontrack.info). Radcliff et al. (2007) also provide an excellent overview of the process and language of creating a rubric.

This activity can be done in collaboration with the faculty member so that she can provide context for the assignments. Also, this is not a circumstance for the librarian to become involved in the grading of the assignment, but rather noting an element of the success or failure of the assignment. As long as this distinction is clear, the librarian and the faculty member can both benefit from the activity. Viewing the actual work of students can give the embedded librarian an insight into the outcome of the course that is unavailable from the other methods.

Gathering LMS Statistics

Your assessment may benefit from the analysis of usage statistics that are captured by the learning management system. All LMS options contain some statistics-gathering capacity, and they all offer at least a rudimentary reporting mechanism. It is a way to collect information on the movement of students around the course site. Course statistics are generally limited to how many times a given page or document was opened or visited. The depth of this information does not give the librarian a complete picture of student activity among the embedded resources in the LMS, but it reveals which students visited areas of the course site and how often they did so. You can at least tell how popular those areas were and perhaps tell when students used them during the length of the course. This can help fill in the gaps that may be left from assessing small samples of survey respondents; 60 percent of survey respondents (say three out of five) might report that they have visited the embedded librarian page in the LMS, but tracking the LMS statistics may show that a higher percentage of the 24 students in the class actually landed on the page. You may not gain a qualitative sense of what students actually did when they looked at your embedded resources, but you at least have a sense of movement around the resources.

An important element of access to course statistics gets back to the issue of what role or status the librarian has in the LMS. Statistics can be limited to the instructor role in some systems (like Blackboard). In cases where statistics are not available to your role, you may be able to request that the instructor provide you with course statistics (at least at the conclusion of the course). It would be interesting to investigate whether students who spent the most time in the embedded librarian's materials did well in the course, or at least to compare page visits with another form of assessment (information literacy assessment scores or assignment analysis). Some restrictions involving students' personal information and grades, notably FERPA (the Family Educational Rights and Privacy Act) regulations, may restrict this data from the librarian, but an anonymous comparison may be able to be done with the cooperation of the faculty member.

Usability Testing

Another method of assessment that is worth mentioning here is that of usability testing. It fits in very well with the expectations of the final phase of the ADDIE model, Evaluate, to provide guidance on how the embedded librarian experience can be modified and improved. Usability testing has as its focus not so much the learning process as in the ease of use of the embedded librarian's materials in the LMS. This type of assessment aims to reveal how well the instructional design and development work of chapter 5 performs with real users of the embedded librarian's resources in the LMS. It is another way (in addition to the methods discussed earlier) to get a glimpse of what students see as they encounter the embedded librarian.

There are some key elements to understand about usability testing as you implement it. First of all, the test should involve real users, or at least people who are members of the target audience of the embedded librarian program, typically students. Second, you should ask the people testing the embedded library resources to complete tasks to confirm that they are not just looking the pages or links over and giving their impressions of them. Third, you need to carefully note what the testers do and say during their interaction with the embedded librarian materials; this information can help you determine where the testers are running into barriers. And that is an important takeaway from this process: the focus is on locating problem areas in the design of the materials rather than being an exhaustive study of what users like or dislike (Norlin and Winters 2002). Approaching this activity from the right point of view will help you design a meaningful usability test.

The method and timing of conducting usability tests for embedded librarianship will vary depending on the tasks you would like to assess, and perhaps the age of the program. A brand-new implementation of embedded librarianship may benefit from some usability testing before it is first offered. More seasoned programs could likewise benefit from revisiting a design that is tried and true from the librarian's perspective, but may still have some gaps for students. It is unlikely that every course offering with an embedded librarian could be usability-tested at any point in the course of a given semester. But every program will have periods where new techniques are introduced, or content is largely revised, and at these points it is wise to establish a set of tasks and recruit some users to give them a try. More information on usability testing is available from various sources, many of which are collected at the "Usability in the Library: Resources" page on the University of Michigan Library site (www.lib.umich.edu/usability-library/usability-library-resources).

Examples of Assessing Embedded Librarian Programs

So how are embedded librarians performing their duties? Is their method of collaborating with faculty, teaching information literacy skills, and interacting with students in the LMS effective? There is no definitive, universally-applicable answer to this as yet, but below are brief synopses of published studies that offer insights into how embedded librarians are impacting their students and faculty. They serve as models of putting assessment to work with embedded librarian courses that can guide further efforts.

The University of Florida

Edwards, Kumar, and Ochoa (2010) describe their experience in offering embedded librarian services in an online graduate course on educational technology. Their research question for their assessment process was, "Does the continued presence of a librarian and weekly library instruction affect students' perceptions and performance of searching skills?" (2010, 280). They collected data using multiple means: (1) a 12-item pre-survey of students' perceptions of their library skills, (2) a post-survey of students' perceptions after completing library research assignments (using the same survey), (3) student responses to questions posted during the course in the librarian-focused discussion forum in the LMS, (4) an interview with the instructor following the completion of the course, and (5) student responses to a discussion forum question at the end of the course. Student perceptions of their experience with library searching and specific library resources increased from the pre-survey to the post-survey between 16 and 30 percent. Responses in the open-ended questions on the survey indicated that the responding students' increase in confidence was due to the presence of the embedded librarians. This assessment was strengthened by the responses to the discussion forum questions and the instructor's interview. In the future, the authors hope to add more quantitative means for assessment.

The Community College of Vermont

Schroeder (2011) details the creation and assessment of an embedded librarian program that grew from 11 courses supported in the first semester of 2004, to 91 courses (split among four librarians) served in the spring of 2010. The institution offers many online courses, which was an initial motivator to create embedded librarian services, and this fact also led to the wide use of Blackboard in face-to-face courses. A variety of factors led the librarians at the college to completely abandon face-to-face information literacy instruction and replace it with a combination of video tutorials and online subject guides for many classes and an increased use of embedded librarians. Their assessment consisted of an institution-wide survey that asked students to agree or disagree with the statement, "Overall, I feel confident using the Hartness Library." In the fall of 2009, one year after face-to-face library instruction was abandoned, 93.8 percent of students agreed with the statement. This result compared well to a prior survey from 2007 in which 68.3 percent of students agreed with the statement. A question on the same survey focused on faculty members' satisfaction with the embedded librarian program, finding that 76 percent of respondents were satisfied. Only 10.7 percent of faculty had not used the service.

George Washington University

Sullo et al. (2012) aimed their assessment toward a proactive redesign of embedded librarian instructional materials. They analyzed questions posed on the Blackboard discussion board by students from 16 online courses that had an embedded librarian. From sorting and then categorizing the questions, they were able to determine which areas of research were causing difficulties for students. Leading the list were navigating off-campus access to library resources, locating books and journal articles, general research skills, and citation management. The next step was to implement real-time instruction sessions with the classes using Elluminate within the LMS. The hope is to proactively equip students with needed information and skills.

Summary

Assessment is a necessary part of the instructional design process that should guide embedded library services. While assessment can be dreaded as the mindless collection of data for the sake of creating statistics and reports that no one pays attention to, it is better to think of assessment as data collection that has a good end—the improvement of your embedded library service. More work in this area needs to be done and then reported in the literature, with embedded librarians using a wider array of methods. Attention must also be paid to establishing the merits of this mode of information literacy instruction.

References

Edwards, Mary, Swapna Kumar, and Marilyn Ochoa. 2010. "Assessing the Value of Embedded Librarians in an Online Graduate Educational Technology Course." *Public Services Quarterly* 6 (2/3): 271–291.

Matthews, Joseph R. 2007. *Library Assessment in Higher Education.* Westport, CT: Libraries Unlimited.

Norlin, Elaina, and CM! Winters. 2002. *Usability Testing for Library Websites: A Hands-on Guide.* Chicago: American Library Association.

Radcliff, Carolyn J., Mary Lee Jensen, Joseph A. Salem, Jr., Kenneth J. Burhanna, and Julie A. Gedeon. 2007. *A Practical Guide to*

Information Literacy Assessment for Academic Librarians. Westport, CT: Libraries Unlimited.

Schroeder, Ann. 2011. "Replacing Face-to-Face Information Literacy Instruction: Offering the Embedded Librarian Program to All Courses." In *Embedded Librarians: Moving Beyond One-Shot Instruction,* edited by Cassandra Kvenild and Kaijsa Calkins, 63–78. Chicago: Association of College and Research Libraries.

Sullo, Elaine, Tom Harrod, Gisela Butera, and Alexandra Gomes. 2012. "Rethinking Library Service to Distance Education Students: Analyzing the Embedded Librarian Model." *Medical Reference Services Quarterly* 31 (1): 25–33.

Westbrook, Lynn. 2001. *Identifying and Analyzing User Needs: A Complete Handbook and Ready-to-Use Assessment Workbook with Disk.* New York: Neal-Schuman Publishers.

Extending Your Reach While Coping with Workload Issues

> I am only one, but I am one. I cannot do everything, but I can do something. And because I cannot do everything, I will not refuse to do the something that I can do.
>
> —*Edward Everett Hale, 1822–1909*

IN THIS CHAPTER:

Workload

Once the LMS embedded librarian program is launched and positive feedback flows, confidence grows. The initial decision was sound and met a perceived need. A conviction to continue and grow the service naturally follows. Simultaneously, workload issues may surface which could jeopardize the service's future, unless addressed thoughtfully. Administrative problem-solving skills must be applied to circumvent any crippling crisis or escalating conflict that might be brewing among library staff. Solutions exist to the potential problems you face in delivering reference assistance and information literacy instruction in LMS courses. Now may be the time to reallocate staff responsibilities and reorganize internal workflow to expand LMS embedded librarianship. Library priorities are flexible rather than fixed, after all. Sharing time, talents, and resources may make the undertaking manageable rather than burdensome.

LMS Embedded Librarian Survey

The national picture of LMS embedded librarianship provides a wider perspective with which to view the local effort. LMS embedded librarianship, based on 280 respondents to the 2011 national survey, is as follows:

- Librarians with embedded librarianship responsibilities (191)—68 percent
- The majority work at four-year universities offering graduate degrees (155)—55 percent
- The second largest group work at two-year community colleges (65)—23 percent
- Librarians currently collaborating with faculty in the LMS (201)—72 percent
- Librarians that have been working from one to three years as embedded librarians (99)—36 percent
- Those embedding in four or fewer course sections per semester (122)—44 percent

Because LMS embedded librarianship services vary among institutions, it is useful to note the most and least popular services:

- Links to library databases and resources (202)—76 percent
- Encouragement to contact the embedded librarian for assistance (203)—76 percent
- Synchronous student chats (37)—14 percent

LMS embedding is nearly the same irrespective of course format:

- Traditional, face-to-face courses (182)—69 percent
- Online courses (184)—70 percent

More librarians embed in:

- Undergraduate courses (160)—61 percent
- Graduate courses (110)—42 percent

Assessment tools vary from most to least used:

- Student surveys (103)—48 percent
- Focus groups of faculty (11)—5 percent

In the next 12 months, most respondents expect their program to increase in terms of the number of courses served per term: (137)—49 percent.

What then do these figures mean? In particular, what do these numbers reveal regarding the challenges embedded librarians face? When given the opportunity to comment freely, survey respondents mention consistent challenges:

- Scalability: time, money, and staffing
- Faculty buy-in: collaboration is necessary
- Resistance: faculty, information technology, administration, and librarians
- Technology: skills, knowledge, and difficulties
- LMS access

Certainly, implementing a new information literacy delivery method is exciting, but it is admittedly difficult. Based on survey feedback, LMS embedded librarianship is expanding where it is being undertaken, yet there seems to be an underlying resistance to the effort. Confront the hard realities but move forward. Sustaining and expanding the program will necessitate change, uncomfortable as that may be for some. Recognize the fear, misconceptions, and resistance to change. Then rethink, reorganize, and rebuild. Based on survey comments, the chief fear can be summarized in the S-word: scalability.

Scalability involves making something that works well at one size operate successfully at other sizes. Design must allow for a large number of potential users.

> It's hard to balance the librarian's time with other responsibilities (teaching, instruction sessions, credit-bearing classes, reference desk, and other duties), and it's hard to meet the growing demand.
>
> *(Survey respondent)*

> According to *A Dictionary of Computing*, unless the application is carefully designed to take account of the interactions that will arise when it is called on to service a large number of users, it may well fail to operate at all, or to operate only with an unacceptable level of service. An application that successfully expands its numbers of supported users is said to be *scalable*.
>
> *(Daintith and Wright 2008)*

Examining Your Progress

As seen in the previous chapter, assessment is a necessary part of growing the LMS embedded librarian program on any campus. As professional expertise and time is channeled in this new direction, it will certainly impact other public and library services. Careful thought must be given to what best serves the needs of campus constituencies at the present and in the future. Remaining relevant requires vigilance and on-going change.

Collecting and Analyzing Data

Such is the national scene of LMS embedded librarianship, but discovering how the program is faring on your campus is of primary importance. Collecting quantitative data based on faculty and student usage will shed light on who uses the LMS embedded librarian service. Which department or program is the biggest user? In this way, the greatest library support can be given to those who have the greatest likelihood of present and future use. Analyze statistics and look for patterns:

- Undergraduates
- Graduates
- Subject discipline
- Lower or upper division
- Traditional, hybrid, or online courses
- Programs: distance learning, first-year experience

Next, examine the qualitative evidence from shared anecdotes as well as comments from e-mails, surveys, forums, focus groups, and the like. What observations and stories have been shared? Listen to what users say or leave unsaid. Determine what conclusions can be drawn regarding:

- Users' expectations
- Users' needs
- Users' frustrations
- Users' research questions
- Users' information literacy abilities
- Users' requests for help
- How often users ask for help
- How many users ask for help
- Which LMS communication tools work best
- Where content ought to be located

These indicators can then be used in planning further enhancement and expansion. Developing the next stage of LMS embedded librarianship at one's institution depends on synthesizing evidence of what works and what does not.

Reporting Results

After collecting and analyzing data for the term or academic year, results can be reported to stakeholders and supporters. Various campus groups should be notified. Obviously, annual reports apprise administrators of the positive impact of LMS embedded librarianship.

In addition, take advantage of opportunities to share results with faculty at scholarly events. Perhaps there is a weekly administrative meeting, monthly faculty tea, or annual week of showcasing scholarship at your institution where it is possible to present. Then, too, your institution's Center for Teaching and Learning may welcome embedded librarians' publishing articles in their newsletter or journal or even a presentation at a meeting. Professional workshops and subject discipline conferences provide further avenues to share findings about the program. In these ways, many potential collaborators and supporters may come to learn about LMS embedded librarianship, better understand the concept, see it as user-friendly rather than threatening, appreciate its added-value, and support its implementation.

Decisions: Which Campus Constituencies?

Based on the literature and embedded experience, it is clear that some departments and programs respond more enthusiastically to LMS embedded librarianship. Providing equitable library resources and services to students enrolled in online or hybrid courses is a driver for this service. Then, too, face-to-face courses that are taught off-campus, and possibly without a library or librarian readily available, are still more reasons to supply equitable access to library collections and assistance. When research assignments comprise a significant part of coursework, then it makes sense to supply reference assistance and resources to students who work in their online course space. Other likely stakeholders who might benefit are those enrolled in courses where there is a capstone project, a thesis or dissertation, a literature review, an annotated bibliography, or graduate research methods' focus.

Given the proper context, students will utilize library content that the embedded librarian supplies. Upper division courses might benefit from having an LMS embedded librarian present as undergraduates are required to search subject-specific databases and electronic collections unfamiliar to them. Difficult research assignments that entail searching scholarly resources unknown to many often frustrate students, who welcome the available expertise of a research consultant within the LMS. In their time of need, often just prior to the due date, students do in fact reach out to the LMS embedded librarian. Then, too, first-year students studying English composition or communication may also welcome the presence of a personal librarian within their course. In these introductory courses, students are learning the research process and correct citation styles as they write papers or deliver speeches. In summary, deciding where to continue embedding or expanding the program at your institution will take some thought.

Workload Implications

Admittedly, scalability is the common concern of those who are planning for or currently involved in LMS embedded librarianship. As noted in the authors' survey, most respondents are facing an increasing demand for the service yet wonder how to deliver a high-quality program, given the limited and even reduced library funds, resources, staffing, and time. Most librarians carry multiple responsibilities rather than this sole responsibility. Then, too, changing technology in the industry and on campus that necessitates troubleshooting or recreating content expends these limited resources. Varying comfort-level and skills with technology among librarians, moreover, can present problems executing an online presence.

Certainly, workload issues do arise and cause concern. Demand on the LMS embedded librarian's time is especially heavy at given points:

- Beginning of term
- Peak periods of use
- Initially creating original content, tutorials, or modules
- Redesigning faculty research assignments
- Grading component of faculty research assignments
- Monitoring discussion board thread questions and comments
- Professors require each student to schedule a research consultation
- Guiding graduate students working on a thesis or dissertation

A fresh and realistic perspective is needed at these times. Invest in making the program sustainable and successful after becoming convinced that LMS embedded librarianship is the preferred approach for students who seldom:

- Come to the library
- Ask questions at the reference desk
- Visit the library website
- Retain what is covered in one-shot library instruction sessions
- Are aware of the wealth of resources academic libraries make available

Be creative yet realistic. As much as one would like, embedding in every LMS course at the same level of involvement is not possible. However, versatility and flexibility are the hallmarks of embedded librarianship; there are workable solutions.

Remember that not all professors expect or require the same level of service. Not all students will utilize the service or individually contact the embedded librarian. The work demand ebbs and flows. Manageable solutions and boundaries can be applied. LMS embedded librarians are problem-solvers and find many ways of working through the issues to solutions.

It is possible to sustain and extend the program. Dismantling the effort is unnecessary. What follows are methods of managing the workload. Some are simple; others are radical. Adopt those that make sense at your institution and proceed.

Workload Models and Solutions

When scalability questions are posed, the hesitant may presume that a 100 percent effort and identical presence must be made available to every instructor, in every course. This is not necessarily true. Various methods of LMS embedded librarianship may be utilized. Certainly, micro-level library courseware involvement is the most labor-intensive as students interact with one librarian who creates customized content. Micro-level embedded librarianship is akin to "made-from-scratch" cooking in that one librarian personally engages students working on their research assignments in a given course site and provides library resources and research advice. Often, this ideal model is the one many envision and rightly worry that they cannot deliver.

> The librarian's involvement is tailored to the needs of the class and can range from providing links to relevant pages on the library website to participating in the creation and grading of

> The decision was made to offer one of two instruction options, embedded or embedded lite, for which a DLT [Distance Learning Team] member would work closely with a research-intensive class, preferably in a subject area in which the librarian specialized.
>
> *(Bean and Thomas 2010, 244)*

> For those I've turned away I created web guides so they would still have some online LI to share with their students.
>
> *(Survey respondent)*
>
> The biggest issue is the growth of the need for embedded librarians without the increase in librarian staff positions. We have been able to maintain this by prioritizing these services and using interns for reference services during peak periods.
>
> *(Survey respondent)*
>
> Faculty wish we could spend more time in their course but it's just not sustainable. We have to pick and choose which courses to be in, typically upper level research methods or courses involving a capstone or thesis project.
>
> *(Survey respondent)*
>
> So we try to pick and choose an appropriate number of courses across our program (e.g., Marketing or Accounting, or Nursing, etc.) where library intervention would work best and be most applicable and thus try to provide enough opportunity for students throughout their program to be exposed to a variety of library skills in preparedness for their completion of their degree.
>
> *(Survey respondent)*

> assignments. The expandability of such an offering is limited as it draws heavily upon librarians' time (Wright and Williams 2011, 7)

However, there are other service options. LMS embedded librarians might adopt a macro-level courseware involvement model that draws upon existing digital objects and resources that can be embedded into LMS courses. Alternatively, embedded librarians might standardize an all-purpose template that provides basic resources and librarian contact information.

> Some content was appropriate for a number of course pages instead of one course, so I made templates to efficiently reuse content for different course pages. For example, I used a template of resources about citation managers on a number of course pages (Haycock and Howe 2011, 158)

Other solutions might be employed involving the contracted time one interacts with students during a term: exclusively at start-up, research segment, or throughout the semester. Yet another approach is to assign one librarian possessing technological and instruction experience the task of creating content to be shared throughout the program, "by creating, collecting, and sharing a library of ready-to-use content for embedded librarians. The goal is to create as much relevant, rich content as possible on a variety of topics and in a variety of formats" (Wright and Williams 2011, 9). Finally, technological solutions by those with LMS and web application development expertise can be utilized. This enables automatic inclusion of the most relevant library subject guide (e.g., LibGuide) or other website within the LMS for every course site, as was done at Duke University for nearly 1,700 course sites by two library staff (Daly 2010).

Boundaries

Given competing responsibilities at work and home, establishing boundaries is necessary. Indeed, healthy boundaries may mean the difference between continuing the service and shutting it down due to exhaustion. Set realistic expectations among end-users. Let them know what level of assistance they may rightfully receive and when you are available to assist them.

- Recognize that your time is valuable and your information literacy skills are needed on campus. Give priority to the courses that include course-related research assignments irrespective of the course format: online, off-campus, hybrid, or traditional.
- Understand that work-life balance is healthy. Let students know how often during the week you monitor the course, what your work schedule is, when you hold office hours (online or in-person), and the typical response time after you receive a request. This is not a 24/7 service. There are other avenues to information literacy available. Build margin into your interactions with users.
- Collaborate initially with willing faculty who will likely promote the service among resistant colleagues. Partner with programs supported by the university that solicit your skills.
- Select the level of support that makes sense. Sometimes a minimalist approach is sufficient. An LMS link to the library website, a subject LibGuide, or a PDF course guide may be all that is needed for many courses. Indeed, these are standard approaches to information literacy. Keep using them. Build more learning objects as time permits.

Referrals

Librarians regularly gather, sort, and file away information to be retrieved when needed. Librarians' strength is knowing where to start searching for needed information, whether in the library collection or at another university department on campus. Since the LMS embedded librarian is an insider in the university system, he is able to make appropriate referrals. This may be the most time-effective solution. Time is a valuable commodity and there may be campus units that are better equipped and funded to handle particular requests. There will be times when directing students to other services on campus makes sense:

- Information technology help desk
- Instructional designers
- Government documents
- Interlibrary loan
- Special collections

- Learning center
- Tutoring
- Writing or math labs
- Faculty subject experts
- First-year programs
- Distance learning
- International students
- Counseling

Standardized Templates

Another approach to maximizing the reach of LMS embedded librarians is to create a standardized template that can be used for numerous courses. Not every course requires custom content. Where more is needed, the template may be adapted. By supplying librarian contact information, links to the library website, a few comprehensive databases, the online catalog, and a citation manager, students have enough to get started. See the research templates designed by Kathleen Pickens, posted to the Miami University Hamilton library website, and used by all the embedded librarians there. You will find examples of common research assignment templates for a persuasive project, speech, literary criticism, etc. (www.ham.muohio.edu/library/niihka).

Reuse and Reposition Content

> "Macro-Level Library Courseware Involvement" . . . Pre-existing content from the library website, such as reference chat service database links, and subject guides, is drawn into the course through automated processes. (Wright and Williams 2011, 7)

Another time-saver is to reuse learning objects as needed. Many such learning objects have already been created at one's institution for one-shot instruction sessions, credit-bearing information literacy courses, and the library website. Often they are saved to an individual's personal server account. Such objects could easily be saved on a shared drive or learning object repository accessible to all LMS embedded librarians. Once digital objects become readily accessible, it is much easier to embed them where most needed. This might include the embedded librarian page, by the research assignment, in a discussion board response to student queries, or e-mailed to the entire student roster.

Here is an example of a frequently used "Citing Sources" page at the Miami University Middletown library website. Embedded librarians harvest what is needed for their various LMS courses. The page includes three learning objects designed by Jessie Long: a comparative chart of five free citation managers and links to two citation LibGuides: *APA Citation Style Guide* and *MLA Citation Style Guide*. Both guides provide examples of popular sources and formats students are likely to cite (www.mid.muohio.edu/library/citingsources.htm).

At Your Library

Investigate what electronic resources, research guides, and tools currently exist at your library and can be incorporated into the LMS embedded workflow. Are there items that might prove useful for students to watch, hear, read, or use? No one insists that material be newly created each time. Linking or copying may be the quick solution. These include:

- Subject and course LibGuides
- Digital tutorials
- PowerPoint or Prezi presentations
- Research mind maps, charts, logs, or rubrics
- Course handouts
- Guides on research concepts
- Posted lists of frequently asked questions
- Blog posts
- Banks of reference questions

Beyond Your Library

Librarians naturally network locally and nationally. The culture of library and information science values resource sharing and empowering users. Librarians champion open-access and open-source solutions. Sharing is what librarians do. Much information and many resources built by others can be incorporated in the work of LMS embedded librarianship. This saves time and money. Do take advantage of material posted to college and university library websites, library consortia holdings, repositories of digital tutorials, and Web 2.0 social networking tools. The sidebar includes a few free offerings to explore.

Excuses: Resistance or Receptivity

> The disappearance of a physical unit for library and information studies was traumatic for many, but the expertise and service remain. (Rudasill 2010, 87)

Each library must embark on the embedded librarian journey after appraising its readiness and balancing it against the institution's need and receptivity. The collaboration and support of key players is critical to successful implementation. Survey respondents recorded comments dealing with buy-in, resistance, and misunderstanding. In the minds of some, the concept of LMS embedded librarianship is an unknown fraught with insurmountable difficulties.

Some university administrators resist the program because they equate it with team teaching that requires additional payment. Some IT administrators resist granting the librarian any access to the LMS, claiming they are not faculty. IT personnel may charge that enrolling a librarian in the role of "instructor" compromises grade book confidentiality. Some professors do not recognize how information literacy impacts student coursework. Faculty may be reluctant to share control of the course or admit their limited knowledge of technology applications and library collections. Some librarians resist assuming new job responsibilities. Some librarians hesitate to admit the inadequacies of their technical skills. They shy away from rather than pursue additional training in the LMS and emerging technologies. Building relationships and trust take time. Take a first step, however small, when ready. Risk is inherent in the change process. Change happens incrementally, one person at a time.

Making Time: Review, Realign, and Stop

Becoming a 21st century academic library entails new ways of thinking and working. Some traditional library tasks and methods have become outdated, inefficient, or costly. It is time to appraise staffing, services, and the infrastructure. Business as usual cannot continue when users are ill-served. Certain solutions must cease so as to free

Apps, E-Books, and Digital Tutorials

- WorldCat–
  www.worldcat.org
- Google Books–
  http://books.google.com
- MERLOT–Multimedia Educational Resource for Learning and Online Teaching–
  www.merlot.org/merlot/index.htm
- ANTS–
  ANimated Tutorial Sharing Project–
  http://ants.wetpaint.com
- YouTube–
  www.youtube.com
- iTunes U–
  www.apple.com/education/itunes-u
- TED Talks–"Ideas Worth Spreading"–
  www.ted.com/talks
- Kahn Academy–2,700 Educational Videos–
  www.khanacademy.org

Citation Generators

- BibMe–
  www.bibme.org
- EasyBib–
  www.easybib.com
- EndNote Web–
  www.myendnoteweb.com/EndNoteWeb.html
- KnightCite–
  www.calvin.edu/library/knightcite
- Zotero–
  www.zotero.org
- Mendeley–
  www.mendeley.com

Information Literacy Assessment

- TRAILS–
  Tool for Real-time Assessment for Information Literacy Skills–
  www.trails-9.org

staff to pursue more meaningful, necessary work, valued more highly by today's stakeholders.

Staffing

Because librarians are highly knowledgeable and skilled, they should be assigned commensurate tasks. Some labor-intensive jobs can be reassigned to support staff, graduate student assistants, and student aides. Some work can be economically outsourced to vendors. Sometimes affordable online solutions can be identified. Some tasks no longer need doing. Realign staff based on their strengths, interests, abilities, and training. Job responsibilities change with the times and technology.

Rethink staffing for maximum impact. Scalability concerns can be turned around. Is it not more cost-effective for an LMS embedded librarian to spend two hours per week on reference work that benefits 100 students working on the same course-related research assignment rather than spend that same amount of time helping a single student at the reference desk? (Figa, Bone, and MacPherson 2009). When it is possible to e-mail weekly research tips to an entire class or post relevant information literacy instruction in a discussion board forum for all one hundred students to read, is this not the more cost-effective approach to reference and instruction?

Many students may hone their search skills when one brave student raises a research question and the LMS embedded librarian replies to all.

> However, one must also consider that the public discussion forum allows all students to benefit from the librarian's work with one student's reference need. For example, the librarian's expended effort to assist one student with a research need can be multiplied many-fold by providing search tips and the strategies used to obtain the results. Other students can then apply these methods to their own information needs. (Figa, Bone, and MacPherson 2009, 93)

Seen in this light, LMS embedded librarianship makes sense and is scalable. Embedded librarianship extends a single librarian's instructional reach. Expertise in academic research is made personally accessible to students who may never have encountered an information specialist.

Web 2.0 Tools: A Few Favorites

- Animoto–Video Slide Showmaker with Music– http://animoto.com
- Audacity–Sound Editor– http://audacity.sourceforge.net
- Bubbl.us–Brainstorm and Mind Map– https://bubbl.us
- Facebook– www.facebook.com
- Flickr–Image and Video Hosting– www.flickr.com
- Glogster–Interactive Poster– http://edu.glogster.com
- Screencast-O-Matic–Screenshots and Screencasts– www.screencast-o-matic.com
- Twitter– http://twitter.com
- Wordle–Word Clouds– www.wordle.net

The library prepared to restructure outreach by developing specific goals for our Embedded Librarian Program:

- Align library services with campus culture.
- Build new relationships and partnerships.
- Increase visibility and approachability.
- Understand student and faculty needs.

(Covone and Lamm 2010, 200)

Undertaking LMS embedded librarianship will involve training. Training may be conducted by library, information technology, or e-learning staff. Beyond the self-starters and volunteers, other librarians may be eased into the LMS service through creative training arrangements like mentoring. At Valdosta State University in 2010, a "buddy system" proved useful in expanding their embedded librarian program.

> Experienced embedded librarians were paired with librarians who were new to the embedded librarian program. One of the librarians was the primary embedded librarian and the other served as a backup when the primary librarian was unavailable. The experienced partner could also provide technical support, answer questions and share his or her experience with the new embedded librarian. (Wright and Williams 2011, 9)

Services

> The most apparent driver for the move to embedded librarianship may be the diminishing budgets that have become unfortunately common for most libraries. Budgetary woes have caused many library administrators to look for new service models in providing library support . . . The concepts that arose from these discussions [at Illinois] seemed to point to the reduction in the forty plus full service units that had been traditionally provided for students and scholars. (Rudasill 2010, 87)

> [L]ibrarians transformed a once overwhelming general sweep of Marshall libraries' many services into a more personal, more manageable endeavor. (Bean and Thomas 2010, 245)

Because teaching and learning are the priorities at your institution, support those endeavors with more LMS embedded librarians. Covone and Lamb emphasize how embedded librarians add value: "By immersing ourselves within not just the course curriculum but also the community and culture, we were able to foster trust and understanding of the library's role in learning" (Covone and Lamm 2010, 199). Reduce professional librarians' responsibilities in other internal activities and areas. Perhaps technical services can be outsourced to a greater extent. Perhaps print, serial, and VHS collections can be weeded or stored off-site in a high-density storage facility. Perhaps acquisitions can be weighted in favor of e-books, full-text databases, and digital multimedia collections of images, music, and videos that can be viewed as clips or in entirety. Establish acquisition profiles with a national jobber like YPB to streamline selection, cataloging, and processing. Undertake special-collections digitization projects so that more users may access these collections. In these ways, a librarian's time is freed and redirected to public services, and more specifically, LMS embedded librarianship.

Rethink public services. How many public services desks are needed? Can circulation and reference be consolidated as one service point? Can other public service desks such as serials, government documents, or instructional media be centralized? At what level should they be staffed? Can library aides, interns, or support staff man these service points and refer users to professional librarians when research or collection questions are asked? With declining reference questions, it is wasteful for a librarian to wait at a desk for users to appear.

Nationally, reference transactions are declining, as the table below indicates:

Reference Transactions, Including Computer Searches, Carnegie Classification, Doctoral/Research

2002	600,459
2004	487,070
2006	309,923
2008	292,535

Source: U.S. Department of Education, National Center for Education Statistics, Academic Libraries Survey (ALS), Table 3, for 2002, 2004, 2006, 2008. http://nces.ed.gov/pubsearch/getpubcats.asp?sid=041#050.

Often these requests can be handled more cost effectively by support staff and library student aides. When the need arises, referrals to professional librarians can be made. Better to work productively and professionally at one's optimal ability and pace. As Rudasill acknowledges, "librarians are becoming more adept at creating guides to the literature in electronic format whether in a subject area or in order to support for specific classes" (Rudasill 2010, 86).

New Directions

Higher education has moved online. Publishing has moved online. Mass media has moved online. Technology prices and device sizes are decreasing. Twenty-first century learners are creative collaborators who live online with all their friends and tools. Librarians must join them there, collaborate with faculty, and continue to develop new technology skills.

That is where and why LMS embedded librarianship is likely to thrive. Our students and faculty work daily in the LMS. If librarians do not show up in their online learning and teaching space, the likelihood of contributing to the central mission of the institution dims. Fewer intellectual interchanges on research will result. Librarians will be seen as distant strangers, costly, and expendable. A new vision of what is important and possible is necessary in the information age.

> A new generation of learners and information users is changing the execution of traditional library services. As the role of the librarian morphs to include a hybrid of skills and duties, the location of library service provision has to change to meet current user expectations. As information exponentially expands along with society's expectation for service, librarians must rise to the occasion and break out of the stereotypical librarian mold.
>
> *(Covone and Lamm 2010, 198)*

Summary

LMS embedded librarians are at the forefront of the learning and teaching mission. Affirm and support this indispensable work. You are productive professionals working with peers to educate students in information literacy, a necessity in the information age. Changing conditions dictate that libraries focus time and training on one thing: instructing students in the research process. Admittedly, the quest looms large and some may become discouraged. This is especially true when other academics, who feel threatened or merely misunderstand the enterprise, place obstacles in your path. Nevertheless, the future of reference and information literacy lies in LMS embedded work. Cease doing no-longer-needed tasks or work that can be accomplished through outsourcing or by well-trained support staff or by referral to more appropriate university offices. It creates more time, a precious commodity.

By sharing the workload of creating learning objects, research templates, LibGuides, HTML pages, websites, and wikis, LMS embedded librarianship is scalable. By showing up online in the LMS as an embedded librarian collaborating with faculty, it is possible to encounter and interact with students struggling with research questions. Although the same level of service may not be feasible or even desirable by all parties concerned, students benefit from access to embedded librarians who are responsive to their research needs. The demand and expectations among faculty and students are not equal, in any case. Providing the essentials within the familiar LMS course will get students started in research. Librarians already staff physical and virtual information desks; build websites where electronic resources, tutorials, and tools reside; and create electronic research guides. It is efficient to reposition these same research links and aids in the LMS—the online environment where students are most apt to find them— next to their course assignment. The service is personal, proactive, and student-centered. It takes the same amount of time to guide one as 101 via the LMS. This is the future. Be there, whatever it takes.

References

Bean, Teresa M., and Sabrina N. Thomas. 2010. "Being Like Both: Library Instruction Methods that Outshine the One-Shot." *Public Services Quarterly* 6 (2/3): 237–249.

Covone, Nicole, and Mia Lamm. 2010. "Just Be There: Campus, Department, Classroom . . . and Kitchen?" *Public Services Quarterly* 6 (2/3): 198–207.

Daintith, John, and Edmund Wright. (n.d.) "Scalability." In *A Dictionary of Computing, Oxford University Press.* www.oxfordreference.com/view/10.1093/acref/9780199234004.001.0001/acref-9780199234004-e-4606.

Daly, Emily. 2010. "Embedding Library Resources into Learning Management Systems: A Way to Reach Duke Undergrads at Their Points of Need." *College and Research Libraries News* 71 (4): 208–212.

Figa, Elizabeth, Tonda Bone, and Janet R. MacPherson. 2009. "Faculty-Librarian Collaboration for Library Services in the Online Classroom: Student Evaluation Results and Recommended Practices for Implementation." *Journal of Library and Information Services In Distance Learning* 3 (2): 67–102.

"Edward Everett Hale." (n.d.) In *The Oxford Dictionary of American Quotations, Oxford University Press.* www.oxfordreference.com/

view/10.1093/acref/9780195168235.001.0001/q-author-00008-00000684.

Haycock, Laurel, and Andy Howe. 2011. "Collaborating with Library Course Pages and Facebook: Exploring New Opportunities." *Collaborative Librarianship* 3 (3): 157–162.

Rudasill, Lynne Marie. 2010. "Beyond Subject Specialization: The Creation of Embedded Librarians." *Public Services Quarterly* 6 (2/3): 83–91.

Wright, Laura B., and Ginger H. Williams. 2011. "A History of the Embedded Librarian Program at Odum Library." *Georgia Library Quarterly* 48 (4): 7–11.

Future Developments in Embedded Librarianship

IN THIS CHAPTER:

Introduction

Embedded librarianship is an established service in academic libraries and continues to add practitioners, as the authors' survey and the increase of articles in the library literature shows. Students are being reached at their point of learning in the place that they access and work on their assignments. Librarians are reaching out and connecting with students and faculty members in a deeper and more nuanced way than they have been able to before. The practice of embedded librarianship has certainly not plateaued, but it has not become a standardized offering either. As such, librarians need to constantly investigate and review what is happening with their programs. What reactions are embedded librarians hearing from their students and faculty? What challenges have they faced as they created embedded services? And what do they foresee for the development of their programs?

Those three questions were asked in the authors' survey of embedded librarians (see appendix for more details). The answers provide some insight into what is happening in embedded library programs worldwide. Together, they should encourage, caution, and inspire the embedded librarian.

There was no shortage of positive comments among the responding librarians (except from those who had just started their programs). Some respondents described the types of comments they had received and others quoted actual comments from students and faculty. While the results do not prove that embedded librarianship is successful, they are indicative of the reactions that librarians are receiving.

A selection of the many comments is provided below (grouped by who provided the comment):

Faculty

- "From a Faculty Survey conducted August 2011: Students had help available beyond what I had the skills to provide and took a load off of me. Students who used service very complimentary and happy to have it. 8/19/11 3:26 PM."
- "We so appreciate your expertise. It makes a huge difference in the course and students' success."

Students

- "Our faculty and students love this service. When asked how he did research, one student said he decided on a topic and then talked with 'His Larry'—the embedded librarian."
- "Student 2010 survey responses: It was very nice to have a librarian like that in our classroom. Especially when we have to find journals."
- "It is great to have your assistance. The course is stronger with your moderating and input."

Librarians

- "It changed my relationship with the students. I went from being just a librarian to being an instructor. I already had a good relationship with the prof, but this made it better—and we were able to work together in a different way."
- "Faculty and students are delighted with the assistance and instruction provided by the librarians. Faculty and students understand that they have, essentially, a 'personal librarian.' Those students who have not had an information literacy session in a previous course are particularly impressed by the knowledge, skills, and techniques shared by the librarians."

The challenges that the survey respondents found in implementing their programs are many. They include limitations placed on current and prospective embedded librarians by budgets, campus IT units, faculty, students, and other librarians. Others (the authors included) feel besieged by time (and the lack thereof). Here is a selection of comments from librarians that serve as examples of the most common types of barriers:

- "The biggest issue is the growth of the need for embedded librarians without the increase in librarian staff positions. We have been able to maintain this by prioritizing these services and using interns for reference services during peak periods."
- "Getting administrative access for our librarians. The main people who oversee Blackboard were hesitant at first to give us administrative access so we could add things to courses. They only gave it to our head of instruction at first and recently more of us have been given access."
- "Getting faculty to let me really become part of the class."
- "Getting students in courses where we are embedded to be aware and take advantage of our service."
- "Librarians who do not want to deal with embedding, either because they feel they are too busy to add it to their workload, or because they are uncomfortable working with the technology involved, or because they are simply frustrated at our university's push into online teaching and view their own refusal to cooperate as 'making a statement.'"
- "Victims of our own success. We can sometimes feel overwhelmed with the amount we do since we have to tailor broad concepts of IL, etc. within the confines of the course topic and schedule. Sometimes faculty want to schedule our times early in the semester before the research project comes near, and we have to work with them to understand that research instruction should come closer in date to the project."

Despite these challenges—some of which are easier to overcome than others—embedded librarians who have programs underway are overwhelmingly positive about their work continuing and growing. When asked their expectations for their embedded programs over the next 12 months, 49 percent (137) of those surveyed said that their program will grow in the number of courses served per academic term. Of the respondents, 37 percent (104) thought that their number of courses would stay about the same. A total of 13 percent of respondents (37) chose "other" as their response, and are likely drawn from the 14 percent (39) who chose "no" or "other" as their response to the question of whether they are collaborating with faculty in the LMS. Only 1 percent (2) believed that their embedded offerings will involve fewer courses per academic term than they did at the time of the survey and zero imagined that their program would cease.

The group of 86 percent of respondents who anticipate that their programs will grow or expand make a case for a strong future for embedded librarianship. In order to continue toward that future, survey respondents shared specific changes they would make to their programs over the next twelve months. Some relate to adding new technologies, others to changing the role of librarians or expanding the scope of their programs. One of the authors' favorite comments could well be the rallying cry of librarianship as a whole: "We will tweak it so it can be sustained." A sampling of the others (all from librarians) is listed below:

- "Not sure yet. Probably do some formal assessment, and work on more of a plan for the program."
- "Plan to have library presence in every DE course. We will be migrating to a new course management system (Moodle), and it's a perfect time."
- "I want to use software like Skype or Elluminate."
- "We've started to use more personal videos to introduce ourselves and do more on-the-fly screencasts using Jing."
- "More marketing/publicity, especially by individual subject librarians to individual faculty members in their subject areas."
- "Well, we aren't planning any changes at this point. However, our student enrollment is up, but we are experiencing a hiring freeze, so we may offer embedded librarians as an alternative to a formal instruction session. We only have eight librarians that do instruction and workload is getting heavier and heavier as enrollment increases and word of mouth spreads."
- "We moved from WebCT to Blackboard this summer and have increased our offerings; I hope we can improve on that this year."
- "We already design tasks related to the student's assignment, which the students answer on the Library forum and we respond to. We plan to embed further in this way."
- "Getting more librarians involved, adopting and integrating new features of our LMS."

- "We are moving toward an across-the-board embedded library instruction model for First Courses. We are also moving toward more authentic assessment of the artifacts produced as a result of our presence and working with the Institutional Research and Analytics group to do a wide-scale persistence study."
- "I'd like to work on embedding more content that we already have created using Libguides and add additional tutorials. I'd also like to see more of a collaboration on the creation of assignments and those assignments being graded. Since this is the first semester anyone has responded to me about this effort I'd like to see how we can make the experience more measurable to make sure we are fulfilling learning outcomes."

As embedded librarianship goes forward, there are several more questions to answer. What trends in society, technology, and education will influence the future of embedded librarians? What can current and potential embedded librarians do to enhance their programs? And how should the practice of embedded librarianship be altered to better meet student information literacy needs? The answers to these questions will guide the daily work of embedded librarians as they shape their programs, survey their institutional environments, and bring further evolution and revolution to the practice of their colleagues.

What Is Coming?

The following four developments are ones you should watch as you plan for the future of embedded library services. They will impact several facets of library work whether or not a given library offers embedded librarianship.

The Growth of Online Learning

Online course enrollment continues to grow. The period from fall 2009 to fall 2010 showed an online enrollment increase of 10.1 percent, while overall enrollment only grew by 0.6 percent (Allen and Seaman 2011). This trend shows no sign of slowing, with 77 percent of higher education institutions offering online courses in 2011 and

54 percent of college presidents predicting that most of their students will be enrolled in an online course in 2021 (Parker, Lenhart, and Moore 2011). As more courses are offered online, librarians will find that providing services to students in these courses is not just an option, but a necessity to reach a growing percentage of their institution's students. Coupling this with the steady growth of the percentage of all courses that make use of the LMS (59 percent of courses in fall 2011, up from 17 percent in 2000 [Campus Computing Project, 2011]) means that librarians will continue to use the LMS to reach courses of all kinds. More online instruction will create both a demand for embedded librarians, but also create the opportunity for them to develop new approaches to providing service. They will seek to apply those approaches as widely as possible, and that will spark more chances to collaborate with faculty in the LMS.

More and More Mobile Students

Mobility is a term that can be used to discuss a number of aspects in society. In this case there are two that overlap and impact students, faculty, librarians, and truly entire institutions. The rise of Internet-capable mobile devices (e.g., smartphones and tablets) has made communications and access to information ubiquitous for everyone in your institution who can afford one. Dahlstrom et al. (2011) report that 55 percent of students own smartphones, and 10 percent own iPads or other tablets. The falling hardware cost of all mobile devices, and particularly the increased use of those which work with WiFi connections and do not require costly monthly data plans, have made the devices much more common on campus (where institution-provided WiFi is typically present) and at home. Once you have a mobile device (the first kind of mobility), you can then carry on a lot of socializing, shopping, recreational browsing, and, most importantly for higher education, educational interactions from wherever you want to, whenever you want to (the second kind of mobility). Dahlstrom et al. (2011) also detail a number of academic tasks that students use their smartphones for, including e-mailing professors (66 percent of smartphone users), looking up information on the Internet outside of class (59 percent), and accessing course websites or syllabi (45 percent). Constant access leads to a constant desire to complete tasks using your device.

These two types of mobility have already caused libraries and other institutional entities to create versions of their websites that work well on smaller mobile screens and text-reference services that allow mobile users to interact with a librarian (160 characters at a time). Of public universities, 55.3 percent had a mobile app for their websites in the fall of 2011 (an increase from the 32.5 percent that had them in the fall of 2010) (Campus Computing Project 2011). Determining what else needs to happen for libraries as a whole is a work in progress, but embedded librarians need to think about how they can be involved in the communications described above. How can embedded librarians present themselves to smartphone users as good resources for search tips and databases? Part of the answer has to be by involving themselves in the spot that students use to access course information: the LMS.

Changes in the LMS

The LMS—the environment that makes embedded librarianship possible—is bound to experience the addition of new tools and upgrade of existing services, wholesale turnover of systems at institutions, and the introduction of new systems. Chapter 2 offered a review of the current LMS market and mentioned some possible changes coming from new vendors. Embedded librarians need to imagine that their LMS products will change in the short- and long-term periods. Some of the changes will come from the normal flow of product improvement and updating, perhaps with opportunities for embedded librarians to provide input into that process. Content posting might be made easier, the discussion board may become easier to search, and the authorizations given to roles may be tweaked. Other changes, such as a mobile LMS app or the ability to text students without a third-party app, may add whole new capabilities to the LMS. Embedded librarians will need to stay aware of these changes and consider how they might use them. They will also need to be ready for larger transitions to occur if their institution adopts a new LMS. Familiarity with the new system cannot only make it easier for the librarian to transition her own embedded service, but also to serve as a resource for faculty, perhaps leading to new embedded opportunities.

Dominance of Born-Digital Resources

As students and faculty spend more time reading and searching for information online, they will come to prefer easily accessible online sources over traditional print resources. Many have already reached this point. This is not news to libraries—many of our library resources are already online and have been readily searched and utilized in this medium for many years. More are certain to follow, with e-books growing in use and print periodical collections completely giving way to online full-text. Pressures and challenges will also come from student preferences for alternative information sources (e.g., Google) and the growth of open-access journals that librarians have to incorporate into their collective knowledge and guide patrons toward. An excellent overview of the current state and evolving future of digital resources in libraries is provided by the Education Advisory Board entitled, "Redefining the Academic Library: Managing the Migration to Digital Information Services" (University Leadership Council 2011), which illustrates that resources are online, students are spending time searching online, and librarians need to be in this milieu to provide guidance.

What Can the Embedded Librarian Do?

Given the current state of embedded librarianship, as outlined in the preceding chapters, and the possible upcoming changes discussed above, how can an embedded librarian persist in her efforts, improve her service, and sustain this vital link for students? The three items that follow in this section provide a game plan for building, modifying, and growing an embedded librarian program.

Stay Current with Embedded Developments

There are a number of ways to watch out for new developments in embedded librarianship. Chapter 3 includes a number of electronic discussion groups, organizations, and conferences that can alert you to new methods or approaches. Judging from several national and regional library conferences that the authors have attended, presentations on embedded librarianship have become an expected part of any broadly themed offering. Another easy way to keep up on publications on the field is to set up search alerts in library databases to send links to newly added articles to you as e-mails or RSS feeds that include the terms "embedded" and "librarian" (check to see how to set this up in your available databases). A related option is to set up a Google Scholar Alert. Just run a search on "embedded librarian" or the terms of your choice and then click on "Create Email Alert" on the Google Alerts page (www.google.com/alerts) to have newly added publications sent to your e-mail. Without dedicated embedded librarian groups in place having regular discussions or physical or virtual meetings, much work is left to individual librarians to network with other embedded librarians or to create some structures (Facebook groups, etc.) that could lead to sustained exchanges of methods, struggles, and successes.

Follow Best Practices

Even in this early stage of embedded librarianship a number of articles have attempted to articulate best practices. More development and explanation of practices is needed, and a broader discussion of them by embedded librarians will help identify useful ones to share. Best practices should not be seen as a list of absolutes that all embedded librarians must follow. They should be consulted, however, to make sure that you are not forgetting something essential as you work with your faculty members and students. To begin, librarians should consult the articles by York and Vance (2009), Hoffman and Ramin (2010), and Burke and Tumbleson (2011). A comparison view of the three lists of best practices is available in table 9.1. The full articles offer additional information on each practice to help you put them to work.

Grow the Service

As with other library instructional services, embedded librarianship needs to grow to reach more students and impact information literacy skills on campus. Chapter 4 covers marketing and chapter 8 covers growing your program; both chapters offer concrete suggestions on increasing the reach of your service. In addition, take the best practices listed above to heart, devise your plan, and then grow the embedded librarian offerings in your library.

What Should Embedded Librarianship Become?

Beyond the individual institutional program or the individual embedded librarian, the larger practice of embedded librarianship needs

TABLE 9.1 A Comparison of Best Practices

York and Vance (2009)	Hoffman and Ramin (2010)	Burke and Tumbleson (2011)
Know the campus CMS and its administrators	Involve other librarians from the beginning	Find faculty who are willing to collaborate
Get a library link in the CMS	Get buy-in from library administration	Find ways to support faculty who are using the LMS or teaching distance learning courses
Go beyond the library link	Market the service to online instructors	Build instructional synergy by combining embedded librarianship with other instructional methods
Don't become overextended—recruit some help!	Clearly negotiate librarian's role with the instructor	Restructure the library so that staff can focus on embedded librarianship
Be strategic with course selection and time	Get information about the class ahead of time	Factor in workload issues created by embedded librarianship
Be an active participant in the class	Be prepared to go outside your subject specialty	Regularly assess embedded librarian efforts
Market the embedded librarian service	Follow up with the instructor	Gain ideas and perspective from collaborating with other librarians
	Plot course assignment deadlines and plan ahead for busy periods	
	Monitor discussion board using e-mail notification or RSS	
	Check courses at set times throughout the day/week	
	Save e-mail messages and discussion board posts for future use	
	Create a library module open to every online student	
	Post embedded librarian's (and subject-specialist's) contact information in the course	
	Post in a single library-specific (or assignment-specific) discussion board	
	Post information proactively	
	Include visuals in discussion board posts	
	Test software and run system check ahead of time	
	Post trouble-shooting tips	
	Be prepared with a "Plan B": have alternatives in place	

to evolve. Embedded librarians should join together to pursue the following three improvements: a larger practitioner community, a research agenda, and a new predominant form of information literacy instruction.

A Larger Practitioner Community

As more librarians work in embedded programs, there will be more ideas created and more ideas shared. Embedded librarianship will be more vibrant and start to replenish itself and make transitions to new technologies ever more smoothly. There is already a solid group of practitioners in place, and they can help bring other librarians into embedded work. If some of the structures of regular communication and conferences are formed, whether initiated by individuals or through associations, it will be easier to create a larger community.

A Research Agenda

Many questions remain unexplored regarding how well embedded librarianship is working and how it is being practiced. The impact of embedded librarian services on student learning and information literacy skills needs to be assessed using more formal studies. There are only a few examples of pre- and post-test assessment comparisons in the literature, and none yet that focus clearly on what role embedded librarianship played in improved scores. Comparisons between students completing tasks in classes that have and classes that lack an embedded librarian also need to be made. Some fundamental work on identifying the prevalence of embedded librarian programs have been completed (see York and Vance [2009] for a survey of embedded librarians in the United States and Corrall and Keates [2011] for a survey of embedded librarians in the United Kingdom). Hoffman (2011) also provides an example of comparing the work of embedded librarians at six institutions. Both further demographic studies and those that attempt to compare services offered at different types of institutions (public and private, community colleges and research universities, etc.) would be useful additions. These suggestions are just the beginning steps in forming a true agenda of topics and projects to research embedded librarians and their efforts.

A New Predominant Form of Information Literacy Instruction

A new standard for information literacy instruction is needed. Face-to-face, 50-plus minute sessions cannot continue as the dominant means of reaching students. As more librarians step up to the challenges of embedded librarianship, they will learn how effective this means of instruction and assistance can be. With a larger practicing group and a clear research agenda, proponents of embedded librarianship can make their case clearly and widely known.

Summary

Embedded librarians must investigate their programs and identify the challenges they have faced, the successes they have achieved, and the changes they hope to make. By staying aware of not only their own programs, but also by investigating barriers and opportunities for embedded librarianship, they can avoid repeating mistakes and find new solutions. With improvements on the individual program level and among embedded practitioners, the practice of embedded librarianship can continue to improve.

References

Allen, I. Elaine, and Jeff Seaman. 2011. "Going the Distance: Online Education in the USA 2011." Babson Survey Research Group. www.onlinelearningsurvey.com/reports/goingthedistance.pdf.

Burke, John, and Beth Tumbleson. 2011. "A Declaration of Embeddedness: Instructional Synergies and Sustaining Practices in LMS Embedded Librarianship." *ACRL*. www.ala.org/acrl/sites/ala.org.acrl/files/content/conferences/confsandpreconfs/national/2011/papers/declaration_embedded.pdf.

Campus Computing Project. 2011. "2011 National Survey of Information Technology in U.S. Higher Education." www.campuscomputing.net/sites/www.campuscomputing.net/files/Green-CampusComputing2011_2.pdf.

Corrall, Sheila, and Jonathan Keates. 2011. "The Subject Librarian and the Virtual Learning Environment." *Program: Electronic Library and Information Systems* 45 (1): 29–49.

Dahlstrom, Eden, Tom de Boor, Peter Grunwald, and Martha Vockley, with a foreword by Diana Oblinger. 2011. *The ECAR National Study of Undergraduate Students and Information Technology, 2011 (Research Report).* Boulder, CO: EDUCAUSE Center for Applied Research. www.educause.edu/ecar.

Hoffman, Starr. 2011. "Embedded Academic Librarian Experiences in Online Courses: Roles, Faculty Collaboration, and Opinion." *Library Management* 32 (6–7): 444–456.

Hoffman, Starr, and Lilly Ramin. 2010. "Best Practices for Librarians Embedded in Online Courses." *Public Services Quarterly* 6 (2/3): 292–305.

Parker, Kim, Amanda Lenhart, and Kathleen Moore. 2011. "The Digital Revolution and Higher Education." *Pew Internet and American Life Project.* http://pewinternet.org/Reports/2011/College-presidents.aspx.

University Leadership Council. 2011. "Redefining the Academic Library: Managing the Migration to Digital Information Services." Education Advisory Board. www.eab.com/Research-and-Insights/Academic-Affairs-Forum/Studies/2011/Redefining-the-Academic-Library.

York, Amy C., and Jason M. Vance. 2009. "Taking Library Instruction into the Online Classroom: Best Practices for Embedded Librarians." *Journal of Library Administration* 49, (1/2): 197–209.

The Embedded Librarian Survey

APPENDIX

The Embedded Librarian Survey was conducted as a web-based survey from September 18, 2011, through October 12, 2011. It was created as a form in Google Docs. The survey was distributed to the following list of library electronic discussion groups, asking librarians to respond anonymously:

- academic_division@sla.lyris.net (Special Libraries Association Academic Division)
- alao@lists.uakron.edu (Academic Library Association of Ohio)
- cjc-1@ala.org (ACRL Community and Junior Colleges Section)
- COLLIB-L@ala.org (ACRL College Libraries Section)
- ili-1@ala.org (ACRL Information Literacy Section)
- infolit@ala.org (American Library Association [ALA] Information Literacy Discussion List)
- LIS-INFOLITERACY@JISCMAIL.AC.UK (Chartered Institute of Library and Information Professionals [CILIP] Information Literacy Group)
- lita-1@ala.org (Library and Information Technology Association)
- OCLSCONF@ls2.cmich.edu (Past and present attendees of the Distance Library Services Conference)
- OFFCAMP@listserv.utk.edu (Association of College and Research Libraries [ACRL] Distance Library Services Section)
- ohiolink@lists.ohiolink.edu (OhioLINK Consortium)

- univers@infoserv.inist.fr (International Federation of Library Associations and Institutions [IFLA] Academic and Research Libraries Section)

A total of 280 librarians responded to the survey. Their responses to each of the 19 question are summarized below.

What is your job title?

The responses ran the gamut from Academic Liaison Librarian to Web Services Librarian. The most popular terms in the job titles were reference (68), instruction (63), director (34), and distance (21).

Is embedded librarianship a part of your responsibilities?

	Number of Responses	Percentage of Total
Yes	191	68%
Other	47	17%
No	42	15%

Choose the following description that best fits your institution:

	Number of Responses	Percentage of Total
4-year university offering graduate degrees	155	55%
2-year community college	65	23%
Other	38	14%
4-year university or college offering only bachelor's degrees	12	4%
University regional campus	8	3%
For-profit institution offering graduate degrees	2	1%
For-profit institution offering only bachelor's degrees	0	0%

Where is your institution located?

Respondents were overwhelmingly from institutions in the United States (219), but responses also came from librarians in Abu Dhabi (1), Australia (1), Canada (10), India (1), Italy (1), Jamaica (1), Malaysia (1), Mexico (1), New Zealand (1), Spain (1), and the United Kingdom (12).

Are librarians at your institution currently collaborating with faculty in the LMS?

	Number of Responses	Percentage of Total
Yes	201	72%
There have been embedded collaborations in the past	23	8%
We hope to start this in the future	17	6%
No	15	5%

Which LMS are you using (or have you used) with embedded courses at your institution?

	Number of Responses	Percentage of Total
Blackboard	145	56%
Moodle	43	16%
ANGEL	36	14%
Other	31	12%
Desire2Learn	26	10%
WebCT	24	9%
Sakai	18	7%

(Respondents were able to select more than one response, so the total percentage will be higher than 100 percent.)

When did you start your embedded librarian program?

	Number of Responses	Percentage of Total
1-2 years ago	50	18%
Over 4 years ago	50	18%
2-3 years ago	49	18%
1 year ago or less	41	15%
3-4 years ago	34	12%
Other	33	12%
N/A	23	8%

How many MLS librarians are employed at your institution?

218 respondents answered this question, listing a total of 2937.4 full-time equivalent (FTE) librarians. That is an average of 13.4 FTE librarians per institution.

How many MLS librarians at your institution are embedded in LMS courses?

218 respondents answered this question, listing a total of 896.4 FTE librarians who are embedded in LMS courses. That is an average of 4.1 embedded librarians per institution. As a whole, embedded librarians make up 31 percent of all MLS librarians at an average institution.

On average, how many individual course sections is each embedded librarian responsible for during a semester?

	Number of Responses	Percentage of Total
4 or fewer	122	44%
Other	65	23%

5-10	53	19%
16 or more	27	10%
11-15	13	5%

What does embedded librarianship include at your institution?

	Number of Responses	**Percentage of Total**
Links to library databases and other information resources within the course	202	76%
Encouragement to contact the embedded librarian for further reference assistance	203	76%
An individual librarian is assigned to one or more participating courses	195	73%
A library tab or link to the library website appears in the LMS for all courses	193	72%
Tutorials, embedded or linked, in the course	184	69%
Information on research concepts (i.e., scholarly vs. popular periodicals, plagiarism, citing sources)	177	66%
Suggested research strategies for course assignments	168	63%
IM or chat widgets in the course	69	26%
Other	58	22%
Interactive sessions with classes using web conferencing software (Adobe Connect, Elluminate, Wimba, WebEx, etc.)	57	21%
Synchronous chats with groups of students	37	14%

(Respondents were able to select more than one response, so the total percentage will be higher than 100 percent.)

What types of courses do you embed in?

	Number of Responses	Percentage of Total
Online or web-based courses	184	70%
Traditional, on-site face-to-face courses	182	69%
Undergraduate courses	160	61%
Hybrid courses (taught part face-to-face and part online)	141	54%
Graduate courses	110	42%
Off-site face-to-face courses	51	19%
Other	15	6%

(Respondents were able to select more than one response, so the total percentage will be higher than 100 percent.)

How do you market your embedded services to faculty?

	Number of Responses	Percentage of Total
Word of mouth—faculty encouraging other faculty	180	70%
Personal invitations by librarians	174	67%
E-mail from librarians	168	65%
Library print brochures or handouts	73	28%
Other	63	24%
Library newsletters (electronic or print)	40	16%
Library blogs	37	14%
Institutional publications	33	13%

Participation is required by department chairs or other administrators	29	11%
Library Facebook pages or accounts	29	11%
Library Twitter accounts	16	6%
E-mails from organizations on campus outside of the library	10	4%

(Respondents were able to select more than one response, so the total percentage will be higher than 100 percent.)

How do you assess your embedded librarian efforts?

	Number of Responses	**Percentage of Total**
Surveys of participating students	103	48%
Other	86	40%
Surveys of participating faculty	71	33%
Analysis of student research assignments	51	24%
Information literacy assessments of students (pre- and post-tests)	44	20%
Focus groups of participating students	12	6%
Focus groups of participating faculty	11	5%

(Respondents were able to select more than one response, so the total percentage will be higher than 100 percent.)

What favorable comments have faculty and students made about the embedded librarian service?

A selection of these comments is included in chapter 9.

What challenges have you had to overcome to implement an embedded librarian program at your institution?

A selection of these comments is included in chapter 9.

In the next 12 months, I expect that our embedded librarian program will:

	Number of Responses	Percentage of Total
Grow in the number of courses served per academic term	137	49%
Stay about the same	104	37%
Other	37	13%
Involve fewer courses per academic term than it does right now	2	1%
Cease	0	0%

How do you hope to change your embedded librarian program in the next 12 months?

A selection of these comments is included in chapter 9.

Do you have any other comments about your embedded librarian experience?

A selection of these comments is included in chapter 9.

Bibliography

Adebonojo, Leslie G. "A Way to Reach All of Your Students: The Course Management System." *Journal of Library and Information Services in Distance Learning* 5 (2011): 105–113.

Allen, I. Elaine, and Jeff Seaman. "Going the Distance: Online Education in the USA 2011." Babson Survey Research Group, 2011. www.onlinelearningsurvey.com/reports/goingthedistance.pdf.

Armstrong, Annie. "Marketing the Library's Instructional Services to Teaching Faculty: Learning from Teaching Faculty Interviews." In *College Libraries and Student Culture: What We Now Know,* edited by Lynda M. Duke and Andrew D. Asher, 31–48. Chicago: American Library Association, 2012.

Asher, Andrew D., and Lynda M. Duke. "Conclusion and Future Research." In *College Libraries and Student Culture: What We Now Know,* edited by Lynda M. Duke and Andrew D. Asher, 161–167. Chicago: American Library Association, 2012.

Asher, Andrew D., and Lynda M. Duke. "Searching for Answers: Student Research Behavior at Illinois Wesleyan University." In *College Libraries and Student Culture: What We Now Know,* edited by Lynda M. Duke and Andrew D. Asher, 71–86. Chicago: American Library Association, 2012.

Association of College and Research Libraries. "Information Literacy Competency Standards for Higher Education." 2000. www.ala.org/ala/mgrps/divs/acrl/standards/informationliteracycompetency.cfm.

Bauwens, Michel. "The Cybrarians Manifesto." *Business Information Review* 9, no. 4 (1993): 65–67.

Bean, Teresa M., and Sabrina N. Thomas. "Being Like Both: Library Instruction Methods that Outshine the One-Shot." *Public Services Quarterly* 6, no. 2/3 (2010): 237–249.

Bell, Steven. J. "The Library Web Site of the Future?" *Inside Higher Education* (blog). February 17, 2009. www.insidehighered.com/views/2009/02/17/bell.

Bell, Steven J., and John D. Shank. *Academic Librarianship by Design: A Blended Librarian's Guide to the Tools and Techniques.* Chicago: American Library Association, 2007.

Bennett, Erika, and Jennie Simning. "Embedded Librarians and Reference Traffic: A Quantitative Analysis." *Journal Of Library Administration* 50, no. 5/6 (2010): 443–457.

Bozeman, Dee, and Rachel Owens. "Providing Services to Online Students: Embedded Librarians and Access to Resources." *Mississippi Libraries* 72, no. 3 (2008): 57–59.

Burke, John, and Beth Tumbleson. "A Declaration of Embeddedness: Instructional Synergies and Sustaining Practices in LMS Embedded Librarianship." Paper presented at Association of College and Research Libraries meeting, March 30–April 2, 2011.www.ala.org/acrl/sites/ala.org.acrl/files/content/conferences/confsandpreconfs/national/2011/papers/declaration_embedded.pdf.

Campus Computing Project. "2011 National Survey of Information Technology in U.S. Higher Education." www.campuscomputing.net/sites/www.campuscomputing.net/files/Green-CampusComputing2011.pdf.

Chesnut, Mary Todd, Threasa L. Wesley, and Robert Zai. "Adding an Extra Helping of Service When You Already Have a Full Plate: Building an Embedded Librarian Program." *Public Services Quarterly* 6, no. 2/3 (2010): 122–129.

Church-Duran, Jennifer. "Marketing Ideas that Work in Academic Libraries." *College and Research Libraries News* 71, no. 8 (2010): 411–412.

Conley, David T. "Rethinking College Readiness." *New Directions for Higher Education,* 144 (Winter 2008): 3–13. doi:10.1002/he.321.

Connaway, Lynn Silipigni, and Marie L. Radford. "Virtual Reference Service Quality: Critical Components for Adults and the Net-Generation." *Libri: International Journal of Libraries and Information Services* 60, no. 2 (2010): 165–180.

Corrall, Sheila, and Jonathan Keates. "The Subject Librarian and the Virtual Learning Environment." *Program: Electronic Library and Information Systems* 45, no. 1 (2011): 29–49.

Covone, Nicole, and Mia Lamm. "Just Be There: Campus, Department, Classroom . . . and Kitchen?" *Public Services Quarterly* 6, no. 2/3 (2010): 198–207.

Cox, Christopher. "Becoming Part of the Course." *College and Research Libraries News* 63, no. 1 (2002): 11.

Cullen, Michael. "Marketing Today's Academic Library: A Bold New Approach to Communicating with Students." *Australian Library Journal* 59, no. 1/2 (2010): 68–70.

Dahlstrom, Eden, Tom de Boor, Peter Grunwald, and Martha Vockley, with a foreword by Diana Oblinger. "The ECAR National Study of Undergraduate Students and Information Technology, 2011 (Research Report)." EDUCAUSE Center for Applied Research, 2011. www.educause.edu/ecar.

Daintith, John, and Edmund Wright. "scalability." In *A Dictionary of Computing, Oxford University Press.* www.oxfordreference.com/view/10.1093/acref/9780199234004.001.0001/acref-9780199234004-e-4606.

Daly, Emily. "Embedding Library Resources into Learning Management Systems: A Way to Reach Duke Undergrads at Their Points of Need." *College and Research Libraries News* 71, no. 4 (2010): 208–212.

Davenport, Tom, and Larry Prusak. "Blow Up the Corporate Library." *International Journal of Information Management* 13 (1993): 405–412.

Dewey, Barbara I. "The Embedded Librarian: Strategic Campus Collaborations." *Resource Sharing and Information Networks* 17, no. 1/2 (2004): 5–17.

Dorner, Jennifer L., Susan E. Taylor, and Kay Hodson-Carlton. "Faculty-Librarian Collaboration for Nursing Information Literacy: A Tiered Approach." *Reference Services Review* 29, no. 2 (2011): 132–140.

Dowd, Nancy, Mary Evangeliste, and Jonathan Silberman. *Bite-Sized Marketing: Realistic Solutions for the Overworked Librarian.* Chicago: American Library Association, 2010.

Drewes, Kathy, and Nadine Hoffman. "Academic Embedded Librarianship: An Introduction." *Public Services Quarterly* 6, no. 2/3 (2010): 75–82.

Duke, Lynda M., and Andrew D. Asher, eds. *College Libraries and Student Culture: What We Know Now.* New York: American Library Association, 2011.

EduTools. 2011. "CMS: CMS Product List." WCET EduTools. www.edutools.info/static.jsp?pj=4&page=HOME.

"Edward Everett Hale." *The Oxford Dictionary of American Quotations, Oxford University Press.* www.oxfordreference.com/view/10.1093/acref/9780195168235.001.0001/q-author-00008-00000684.

Edwards, Mary, Swapna Kumar, and Marilyn Ochoa. "Assessing the Value of Embedded Librarians in an Online Graduate Educational Technology Course." *Public Services Quarterly* 6, no. 2/3 (2010): 271–291.

"Empowering American's Voters—Information Literacy." *National Forum on Information Literacy.* October 2, 2001. www.pr.com/press-release/357922.

Farmer, Leslie S. J. *Instructional Design for Librarians and Information Professionals.* New York: Neal-Schuman Publishers, Inc., 2011.

Figa, Elizabeth, Tonda Bone, and Janet R. MacPherson. "Faculty-Librarian Collaboration for Library Services in the Online Classroom: Student Evaluation Results and Recommended Practices for Implementation." *Journal of Library and Information Services In Distance Learning* 3, no. 2 (2009): 67–102.

Germano, Michael A. "Narrative-Based Library Marketing: Selling your Library's Value during Tough Economic Times." *Bottom Line: Managing Library Finances* 23, no. 1 (2010): 5–17.

Hartness Library. "CCV's Embedded Librarian Program." http://youtube/NZqI1b2bJcI.

Haycock, Laurel, and Andy Howe. "Collaborating with Library Course Pages and Facebook: Exploring New Opportunities." *Collaborative Librarianship* 3, no. 3 (2011): 157–162.

Head, Alison J., and Michael B. Eisenberg. "Assigning Inquiry: How Handouts for Research Assignments Guide Today's College Students." Project Information Literacy Progress Report, University of Washington's Information School. July 13, 2010. http://projectinfolit.org/pdfs/PIL_Handout_Study_finalvJuly_2010.pdf.

Head, Alison J., and Michael B. Eisenberg. "College Students Eager To Learn But Need Help Negotiating Information Overload." *Seattle Times,* June 3, 2011. http://seattletimes.com/html/opinion/2015227485_guest05head.html.

Head, Alison J., and Michael B. Eisenberg. "Lessons Learned: How College Students Seek Information in the Digital Age." *Project Information Literacy First Year Report with Student Survey Findings, University of Washington's Information School.* December 1, 2009. http://projectinfolit.org/pdfs/PIL_Fall2009_finalv_YR1_12_2009v2.pdf.

Head, Alison J., and Michael B. Eisenberg. "Truth Be Told: How College Students Evaluate and Use Information in the Digital Age." Project Information Literacy Progress Report, University of Washington's Information School, November 1, 2010. http://projectinfolit.org/pdfs/PIL_Fall2010_Survey_FullReport1.pdf.

Hill, Phil. "New Mentality Enters LMS Market." Delta Initiative. www.deltainitiative.com/index.php/phils-blog/70-new-mentality-enters-lms-market.

Hoffman, Starr. "Embedded Academic Librarian Experiences in Online Courses: Roles, Faculty Collaboration and Opinion." *Library Management* 32, no. 6/7 (2011): 444–456.

Hoffman, Starr, and Lilly Ramin. 2010. "Best Practices for Librarians Embedded in Online Courses." *Public Services Quarterly* 6, no. 2/3 (2010): 292–305.

INFOhio's 21st Century Learning Commons. "Are You Preparing Your Students for Their Future? Are You Up-To-Speed?" *21 Essential Things for 21st Century Success* no. 1 (2010). http://learningcommons.infohio.org/index.php?option=com_content&view=article&id=78&Itemid=92.

Jennings, Eric, and Kathryn Tvaruzka. "Quick and Dirty Library Promotions That Really Work." *Journal of Library Innovation* 1, no. 2 (2010): 6–14.

Kamkwamba, William, and Bryan Mealer. *The Boy Who Harnessed the Wind: Creating Currents of Electricity and Hope.* New York, William Morrow, 2009.

Keener, Molly, Joy Kirchner, Sarah Shreeves, and Lee Van Orsdel. "10 Things You Should Know About . . . Scholarly Communication," Association of College and Research Libraries. Last modified April 6, 2011. www.ala.org/acrl/sites/ala.org.acrl/files/content/issues/scholcomm/docs/sc101-things.pdf.

Kesselman, Martin A., and Sarah Barbara Watstein. "Creating Opportunities: Embedded Librarians." *Journal of Library Administration* 49, no. 4 (2009): 383–400.

Kolowich, Steve. "What Students Don't Know." *Inside Higher Ed,* August 22, 2011. www.insidehighered.com/layout/set/print/news/2011/08/22/erial.

Konieczny, Alison. "Experiences as an Embedded Librarian in Online Courses." *Medical Reference Services Quarterly* 29, no. 1 (2010): 47–57. Kotler, Philip, and Nancy Lee. 2007. *Marketing in the Public Sector: A Roadmap for Improved Performance.* Upper Saddle River, NJ: Wharton School Publishing.

Kotler, Philip, Hermawan Kartajaya, and Iwan Setiawan. *Marketing 3.0: From Products to Customers to the Human Spirit.* Hoboken, NJ: John Wiley and Sons, 2010.

Leboff, Grant. *Sticky Marketing: Why Everything in Marketing Has Changed and What to Do about It.* London: Kogan Page, 2011.

Lipscomb, Carolyn E. "Clinical Librarianship." *Bulletin of the Medical Library Association* 88, no. 4 (2000): 393–396.

Mathews, Brian. *Marketing Today's Academic Library: A Bold New Approach to Communicating with Students.* Chicago: American Library Association, 2009.

Matthews, Joseph R. *Library Assessment in Higher Education.* Westport, CT: Libraries Unlimited, 2007.

Miller, Susan, and Nancy Murillo. "Why Don't Students Ask Librarians for Help?: Undergraduate Help-Seeking Behavior in Three Academic Libraries." In *College Libraries and Student Culture: What We Now Know,* edited by Lynda M. Duke and Andrew D. Asher, 49–70. Chicago: American Library Association, 2012.

Moeller, Susan, Joseph Ammu, Jesus Lau, and Toni Carbo. "Towards Media and Information Literacy Indicators." November 4–6, 2010. United Nations Educational, Scientific and Cultural Organization. www.unesco.org/new/fileadmin/MULTIMEDIA/HQ/CI/CI/pdf/unesco_mil_indicators_background_document_2011_final_en.pdf.

Montgomery, Susan E. "Online Webinars! Interactive Learning Where Our Users Are: The Future of Embedded Librarianship." *Public Services Quarterly* 6, no. 2/3 (2010): 306–311.

Norlin, Elaina, and CM! Winters. *Usability Testing for Library Websites: A Hands-on Guide.* Chicago: American Library Association, 2002.

OCLC. "The Library Brand 2010." OCLC Perceptions of Libraries, 2010: Context and Community. Dublin, OH: OCLC. www.oclc.org/reports/2010perceptions/2010perceptions_all.pdf.

Oder, Norman, and Lynn Blumenstein. "Personal Librarian Program at Drexel University." *Library Journal* 135, no. 16 (2010): 14.

"Online Learning: By the Numbers." *Chronicle of Higher Education,* 57, no. 11 (November 5, 2010): B28-B29.

Owen, Patricia, and Megan Oakleaf. 2008. "*Using Evidence to Bridge the 12–13 Gap: What College Faculty Say Freshmen Students Don't Do.*" Paper presented at the 34th Annual Conference of the Academic Library Association of Ohio. www.infowen.info/college%20checklist.pdf.

Parker, Kim, Amanda Lenhart, and Kathleen Moore. "The Digital Revolution and Higher Education." *Pew Internet and American Life Project.* 2011. http://pewinternet.org/Reports/2011/College-presidents.aspx.

Pink, Daniel H. *A Whole New Mind: Moving from the Information Age to the Conceptual Age.* New York: Riverhead Books, 2005.

Pravikoff, Diane S., Annelle B. Tanner, and Susan T. Pierce. "Readiness of U. S. Nurses for Evidence-Based Practice." *American Journal of Nursing* 105, no. 9 (2005): 40–51.

Radcliff, Carolyn J., Mary Lee Jensen, Joseph A. Salem, Jr., Kenneth J. Burhanna, and Julie A. Gedeon. 2007. *A Practical Guide to Information Literacy Assessment for Academic Librarians.* Westport, CT Libraries Unlimited.

Redish, Janice (Ginny). 2007. *Letting Go of the Words: Writing Web Content that Works.* San Francisco: Morgan Kaufmann Publishers.

Rudasill, Lynne Marie. "Beyond Subject Specialization: The Creation of Embedded Librarians." *Public Services Quarterly* 6, no. 2/3 (2010): 83–91.

Schroeder, Ann. "Replacing Face-to-Face Information Literacy Instruction: Offering the Embedded Librarian Program to All Courses" In *Embedded Librarians: Moving Beyond One-Shot Instruction.* Edited by Cassandra Kvenild and Kaijsa Calkins, 63–78. Chicago: Association of College and Research Libraries, 2011.

Shumaker, David, and Laura Ann Tyler. 2007. "Embedded Library Services: An Initial Inquiry into Practices for Their Development, Management, and Delivery." Paper presented at the Special Libraries Association Annual Conference, Denver, CO, June 6, 2007. www.sla.org/pdfs/sla2007/ShumakerEmbeddedLibSvcs.pdf.

Strickland, A.W. "ADDIE." Idaho State University College of Education, Science, Math and Technology Education. http://ed.isu.edu/addie/index.html.

Sullo, Elaine, Tom Harrod, Gisela Butera, and Alexandra Gomes. "Rethinking Library Service to Distance Education Students: Analyzing the Embedded Librarian Model." *Medical Reference Services Quarterly* 31, no. 1 (2012): 25–33.

"Team Teaching with an Embedded Librarian." 2008. *Distance Education Report* 12, no. 17 (2008): 6–7.

Thomsett-Scott, Beth, and Patricia E. Reese. "Changes in Library Technology and Reference Desk Statistics: Is There a Relationship?" *Public Services Quarterly* 2, no. 2/3 (2006): 143–165.

Tyron, Jodi, Emily Elizabeth Frigo, and Mary Kathleen O'Kelly. "Using Teaching Faculty Focus Groups to Assess Information Literacy Core Competencies at University Level." *Journal of Information Literacy* 4, no. 2 (2010): 62–77.

University Leadership Council. 2011. "Redefining the Academic Library: Managing the Migration to Digital Information Services." Education

Advisory Board. www.educationadvisoryboard.com/pdf/23634-EAB-Redefining-the-Academic-Library.pdf.

Walters, Suzanne. *Library Marketing That Works.* New York: Neal-Schuman Publishers, 2004.

Weiner, Sharon A. "Information Literacy: A Neglected Core Competency." *EDUCAUSE Quarterly* 33, no. 1 (2010): 8.

Westbrook, Lynn. *Identifying and Analyzing User Needs: A Complete Handbook and Ready-to-Use Assessment Workbook with Disk.* New York: Neal-Schuman Publishers, 2001.

Wright, Laura B., and Ginger B. Williams. "White Paper: A History of the Embedded Librarian Program at Odum Library." *Georgia Library Quarterly* 48, no. 4 (2011): 7–11.

Yarmey-Tylutki, Kristen. "When Students Go Mobile." *Pennsylvania Library Association Bulletin* 65, no. 4 (2010): 13–15.

York, Amy C., and Jason M. Vance. "Taking Library Instruction into the Online Classroom: Best Practices for Embedded Librarians." *Journal of Library Administration* 49, no. 1/2 (2009): 197–209.

Index

A

M

N

O

P

Q

R

S